COACHING
WITH
THE
SCRIPTURES

By Gerald Davis

PRESS

Coaching With The Scriptures
by Gerald Davis

Printed in the United States of America

ISBN 978-1-60647-782-3

COVER DESIGN BY KIRK Q BROWN
WWW.SIGNSANDWONDERSPROMOTIONS.COM

www.xulonpress.com

TABLE OF CONTENTS

High Fives ix

Dedication xi

Acknowledgments xiii

Assists xv

Introduction xix

Preface xxi

1st QUARTER: Offense ... being in the attack mode 23

- Beliefs 24
- Commitment 27
- Dignity 33
- Discipline 36
- Gracious 40
- Integrity 42
- Leadership 45
- Loyalty 49
- Obedience 52
- Student 56

- Trailblazer 58
- Upsets 61

2nd QUARTER: Rebounding ... from mistakes 67

- Choices 68
- Compassion 70
- Favorites 73
- Mistakes 77
- Patience 81
- Rebuilding 84
- Second Chances 87

HALFTIME (Photos) 91

3rd QUARTER: Ball handling ... Cousey, Kidd, Magic, and Nash all rolled into one 97

- Endurance 98
- Faith 101
- Jobs 104
- Organization 106
- Power 109
- Replacements 111
- Scout/Scouting 114
- Strategy 117
- Teamwork 120

4th QUARTER: Passing ... it's better to give than to receive 125

- A Coach's Wife 126
- Conviction 130
- Encouragement 133
- Friends 136
- Fundamentals 139
- Fun/Laughter 142

- Love 146
- Openness 149
- Praise 153
- Respect 157
- Rules 159
- Worship 161

OVERTIME: Free throws ... knock them down **165**

- Anger...166
- Attitude 168
- Bitterness..171
- Deception 173
- Rebellion 176
- Selfishness..179

ABOUT THE AUTHOR..**183**

HIGH FIVES

" "This book is a must read for parents, teachers, and coaches. Coach Davis hones in on important strategies for building better communication in the workplace and home. Read this book and maximize the seen and unseen potential of those you interact with."
- Cyril Parris, Retired Police Lieutenant and Basketball Official

"Your library must contain *Coaching with the Scriptures*. Whether you're a career coach or an aspiring coach, you will learn something new, I promise you!"
- Daniel Nigro, Jr., Men's Basketball Coach

"The calling of a coach is an extremely important component in the kingdom of God, if you're serious about the lives of young people please read *Coaching with the Scriptures*."
- Tom Flynn, Girl's Basketball Coach

"Nothing but net! Coaches, athletes, and educators through university level will find that this intensely practical guide to sportsmanship reveals that true winners bring their relationship with God's Word into their game!"
- Laurie B. Midgette, Educator

"Gerald's Christian message added to the good coaching message will make a different and worthwhile contribution to young and aspiring athletes."
- Rachelle Legions, New York City Schoolteacher/Administrator

"In basketball, it's often mentioned that the point guard should be an extension of the coach on the court. More so, the coach should be an extension of Christ for the team. *Coaching with the Scriptures* brings me closer to obtaining that vision in my walk with Jesus Christ."

- Isaac Wade, Former Player

"What I enjoyed about Gerald's book was that it's practical – simple X's and O's to guide every coach through every situation on and off any court."

- Hugh Flaherty, Girl's Basketball Coach

DEDICATION

To my Dearest Digna,

You continue to be my inspiration.

I will always love you.

ACKNOWLEDGMENTS

To my Lord and Savior Jesus Christ ... Your grace is sufficient ... Your blessings are bountiful ... Your love for me is undisputable!

To my wonderful children – Christina, Bryan, and Brandon – I love you! To my parents – Ottis and Gloria Davis – you are the best! Brother Dwight Davis, Sister Carla Hlyton

To my goddaughter Renee Stoner – you are loved. To my pastor Rev. A. R. Bernard and Elder Karen Bernard – thank you for teaching the nation and me to dream big.

To the coaches who gave me my start in basketball – Ted Gustus, Jr., Todd Jamison, and Daniel Nigro, Jr. – words can't express my appreciation for you.

To friends who offered insight and encouragement during the writing of this book – Anthony Anderson, Laurie Midette, Joan Brown, Julie Akinola, Sherman Roberson, and Roxane Wilson – thank you so much; and to my editor, Janet Angelo, many thanks; the care and detailed attention you've given to this book is invaluable.

To my coaching fraternity who contributed to this project – continue to make an impact on the lives of the young people of this generation!

ASSISTS

Bobbi Jo Austin
Former Assistant Coach,
C. W. Post University, Greenvale, NY

Renee Bostic
Head Women's Basketball Coach
Robert Morris College, Chicago

Kelli Cofield
Assistant Women's Basketball Coach
Nicholls State University, LA

Mark Coluccio
Fitness Trainer
Rockville Centre, NY

Robert Dinardo
Head Women's Basketball Coach
Concordia College, NY

Mike Eisenberg
Head Varsity Girl's Basketball Coach
Francis Lewis H. S., Queens, NY

Wylie Gober
Former Freshman Boy's Basketball Coach
Rice H. S., New York, NY

Seth Goodman
Head Women's Basketball Coach
Monroe College, Bronx, NY

Kathy Gray
Head Varsity Girl's Basketball Coach
Valley Stream H. S., Valley Stream, NY

Eddie Grezensky
Head Varsity Girl's Basketball Coach
Murray Bergtraum H. S., New York, NY

Joe Gugliero
Women's Basketball Coach
A.A.U. High School, New York, NY

Terri Gugliero
Spouse of Joe Gugliero
Women's Basketball Coach

Otis Henderson
Athletic Director
Christian Cultural Center, Brooklyn, NY

Gordon Miles
Basketball Official, New York

Robert Mitchell
Women's Basketball Coach
A.A.U. High School, New York, NY

Deirdre Moore
Assistant Women's Basketball Coach
C. W. Post University, Greenvale, NY

Brenda Morgan
Former Head Varsity Girl's Basketball Coach
Abraham Lincoln H. S., Brooklyn, NY

Deborah Mortley
Head Varsity Girl's Basketball Coach
Bishop Loughlin Memorial H. S., Brooklyn, NY

Anna Nigro
Spouse of Daniel Nigro
Men's Basketball Coach

Ed Nixon
Former High School Basketball Coach
Mississippi

Paul Nixon
Head Women's Basketball Coach
Columbia University, New York, NY

Brad Oringer
Assistant Men's Basketball Coach

Thomas Schiavo
Head Football Coach
Valley Stream North H. S., Valley Stream, NY

Andy Stampfel
Head Men's Basketball Coach
The City College of New York, NY

Pat Torney
Head Varsity Boy's Baseball and Basketball Coach
Newtown H. S., Queens, NY

INTRODUCTION

D o you want to become a better coach? Coaching with the scriptures is a practical guidebook of biblical scriptures and experiences that is geared to help the novice and the professional. Whether you're a coach, parent, or educator, the Bible is filled with powerful and relevant truths that will enhance your skills as a teacher and ambassador of your given sport. *Coaching with the Scriptures* can also be used as a daily devotional to start the day of any busy individual.

Basketball – Football – Baseball – Soccer: It doesn't matter which one is your chosen sport. The Word of God works for any sport, but only if you work the Word.

What's in the book:

- **One word** can tell a story, and in this book a single word will head each section as a way to examine a biblical character and a character trait. Studying their life experiences will help us in our own Christian walk and coaching experience.

- **The Coaches' Corner** – Coaches with years of experience and excellent reputations for integrity will offer practical insight on how to handle various issues that will confront coaches at each level of competition.

- **3-Pointers** – The Bible is our guide and source of conduct for every situation, even in the culture of sports. The three scriptures that will be provided for each sub-topic will highlight and make bold-print impressions of what God is saying about that particular word. These scriptures have been carefully chosen so that you, your family, and your team can walk in victory regarding that area in your lives.

- **Buzzer Beaters** – This section will provide quotes from the famous and the "not so famous," but it will also offer positive insight that connects with the subject matter being discussed.

- **Post-Game Notes** – This section will give you the opportunity to write notes, thoughts, and ideas as you read each chapter.

PREFACE

I can still clearly remember what it was like growing up on East 93rd Street in Brooklyn, New York. And even though I could only go from one corner (Winthrop) to the next (Rutland Road) during my younger years, those were some of the most cherished moments of my childhood. Within that block, our "crew" – Peter and Johnny Cuffe, Anthony Lloyd, Tony Brown, James Prime, and my brother Dwight Davis – had the time of our lives. We played punch ball, baseball, football, and basketball from sunup until 7:00 pm, and then I wasn't allowed to leave my porch. We didn't live in the suburbs so we didn't have the standard basketball hoop hanging from the end of a detached garage, so we used a garbage can for a hoop with Ms. Lloyd's iron driveway gate as the perfect backboard. That's how we learned to play the games we loved. We all went on to play the following sports in high school and some of us in college: Dwight, Peter, and Johnny (Track), James and Tony (Football), Anthony and myself (Basketball). Our boyhood passion for these games could not be quenched; we just loved sports.

It wasn't until high school that I received Jesus Christ as my personal Lord and Savior. It was during those developmental years that my love for God outgrew my love for basketball. I understood more and more about balance: having God-time in my life as well as playtime.

The foundation of my faith was built at a small storefront church called the Triumphant Full Gospel Assembly. The pastors were

Harold Joseph and Eleanor Joseph. During those years I taught Sunday school, worked with the young adults, and was ordained as a deacon. Life was good, because Jesus was at the forefront of my life.

It was later at my new church home – the Christian Cultural Center, pastored by Rev. A. R. Bernard – where I would hear a message that would change my life. It was about pursuing your passion, and for me basketball had always played a big part in my passion for living. During that period in my life my vocation was working as a correctional officer with the NYC Department of Corrections. However, I always knew that I wanted basketball to play a greater role in my life, especially since my competitive playing days had been curtailed due to a knee injury.

That's when a friend of mine, Ted Gustus, Jr., got me an opportunity to coach with a local boy's varsity high school team. That was just the opportunity I needed to begin my second career as a basketball coach, a career that would allow me to follow my passion.

With the experience that I have garnered in basketball and with my love for God and His unadulterated Word, I wanted to integrate the Bible and the teachings of Jesus Christ in such a way that coaches on every level could utilize God's truths in a practical ways to teach their players on various subjects that affect us on our courts and in life. My purpose for writing this book is to pass on some basic principles that will allow the reader to be a positive influence in the culture of sports. My prayer is that the lives of all who read this book will be impacted for God's glory.

1ˢᵗ QUARTER:

Offense ... being in the attack mode

The offensive sets and style of play that a coach or team will implement depends on the players and their capabilities. As a coach, I personally try to recruit players who are athletic, quick, and who like to run. I enjoy a fast-paced game where the players are constantly moving. Three players who remind me of this style are John Havlicek, formerly of the Boston Celtics, Reggie Miller, formerly of the Indiana Pacers, and Richard "Rip" Hamilton of the Detroit Pistons. The defenders who were assigned to guard them on any given night surely earned their money. The mindset of each one of these offensive players was to always be in the "attack mode."

God wants His children to be on the offensive as well. What He doesn't want is for us to be like a defensive player who backpedals, which doesn't place that player in a position of power. You are at the mercy of the offensive player. God has equipped His children – those who are believers in Christ – to be like that offensive player. In reality that's the way we should always be, because Satan takes it as his personal responsibility to keep us two steps behind. In Ephesians 6:11-17, God reminds us to "put on the whole armor so that you will be able to stand safe against all strategies and tricks of Satan." This section of the book, the 1ˢᵗ Quarter, outlines some of the very qualities that Christ desires for the 21ˢᵗ century coach to have.

I have a very competitive nature; to put it simply, I just *don't* like to lose. Just thinking that Satan sets his traps for us to fall into

– thus facing the possibility of losing – makes me want to commit a really hard and aggressive flagrant foul on him.

When I do fail or come short of God's expectations of me, it cannot be because of my lack of preparation or equipment. Therefore, my dear brothers and sisters –in –Christ, STAY IN THE ATTACK MODE!

BELIEF ... *that which is held to be true*

Read: Genesis 6:1-22

Key Verse: Genesis 6:22 – *And Noah did everything as God commanded him.*

Sometimes to a fault, coaches believe so much in their teams that they are not quick to make necessary changes in rosters or a player's minutes. Even so, I would rather be accused of believing too much in my team or player than not enough. As a coach you want to demonstrate as much confidence in your team as possible, not only for their benefit as individual players, but also for their growth and development as productive members of society.

Some players come from a family household or environment filled with discouragement and unbelief, and then they're subjected to the same circumstances and pressures in the gym while being coached. We can't control the environment kids come from, but we can control what sort of coaching environment we establish. The gym is a place that most players consider to be a sanctuary or a place of escape. The coach, therefore, is in a great position to be that special person who has a positive influence on his or her players' young lives and who can instill them with self-worth, confidence, and the empowering knowledge that somebody important believes in them.

In the Bible, Noah listened to enough doubt and unbelief to last a lifetime. Considering he lived to be 950 years old, that's quite a bit. His intestinal fortitude was that of ten men. Noah was a faithful and obedient man who had no trouble sticking to a project. He wouldn't allow the negative conversation of men to sway him from doing what God told him to do. His belief in God was unshakable and immovable. In reading the story of Noah, keep in mind that he wasn't instructed to just go around the corner and pick up a loaf of bread and a dozen eggs. Noah was told to build an ark and then to collect two animals of each species, a male and female of every kind of animal, reptile, and bird. God had decided to destroy all the inhabitants of the earth with a great flood, because after 120 years of second chances, God had grown tired of the same act from disobedient sinners. God hates sin, and His judgment of mankind was enforced through sending the flood. The rains came down strong for 150 days. The only people who were excluded from God's wrath were Noah, his wife, his sons, and their wives.

Noah is an excellent example of good things happening to a good person when they believe God is the only thing that matters. In observing Noah's unquestioning obedience, I'm sure that God must've experienced something that is always a good feeling for a coach – that is, when you believe in a person and then that individual or team comes through with flying colors. It makes the accomplishment that much sweeter. For Noah, his reward was life.

Prognosticators who begin their preseason editorials with predictions of doom can halt a season before it even begins. If you left it up to most of them, it wouldn't be necessary for most players to even tie the laces on their sneakers. As a coach I understand that a team of winners is not based on the definition assigned to them by others and what they believe (or, more often than not, don't believe). All that matters is what the coach and the team believe about themselves.

THE COACHES' CORNER

QUESTION AND ANSWER SESSION FEATURING:

Eddie Grezensky, Head Varsity Girl's Basketball Coach, Murray Bergtraum H. S., New York, NY

Gerald Davis: To be successful, a firm belief in the system must resonate among players and staff. What are some of your core values that you believe are a must for a winning team?

Eddie Grezensky: I believe that you must be willing to work hard in practice. You must believe in the system that we are running – it has worked for previous teams (who have won championships), and it will work for you. You must be willing to compete. You are entitled to an opportunity to compete, and you must make the most of your opportunity.

3-POINTERS

Psalm 18:30 (KJV) – As for God, his way is perfect: the word of the Lord is tried: he is a buckler to all those that trust in him.

Galatians 6:9 (NIV) – Let us not become weary in doing good, for at the proper time we will reap a harvest if we do not give up.

Romans 8:25 (NLT) – But if we look forward to something we don't have yet, we must wait patiently and confidently.

BUZZER BEATER

Faith is the daring of the soul to go further than it can see.
- William Newton Clark

POST-GAME NOTES

....
....
....
....
....
....
....

COMMITMENT ... *the state of being obligated or emotionally impelled to a cause; an agreement or pledge*

Read: Ezra 7:6-10

Key Verse: Ezra 7:10 (NLT) – *This was because Ezra had determined to study and obey the laws of the Lord and to become a Bible teacher, teaching those laws to the people of Israel.*

Whatever you do, do it as if you're doing it for God. No matter what the assignment or task God wants you to accomplish, be the best at it. The world needs to see 100% effort and commitment from you. We are Christ's ambassadors, and we should take pride in how we represent our Savior. Someone is always watching; therefore, give those individuals something good to talk about, not only who you are as a coach but as a true man or woman of God. This can only be done if you're committed to what you do, and it shouldn't be totally about "the money." Now don't get me wrong, money is good. But it cannot be our sole reason for committing to any project or position.

Ezra was definitely an individual who was committed to the pure Word of God. He was a scribe (teacher) whose only desire was to serve God in an extraordinary manner. He understood the Law and loved teaching it; more importantly, however, he was committed to fulfilling and obeying the Word.

The Word of God is alive, powerful, and vibrant, but only if the reader allows it to be so. The Bible was written over 2,000 years ago, and all of the issues that existed during biblical times still confront many of us today. That's right. You cannot escape good or bad experiences! The Bible is like a map or a point of reference. By using it effectively, it keeps us from duplicating the mistakes of our forefathers.

God respected Ezra's abilities as a teacher of the Word so much that He was in favor of Ezra's returning to Jerusalem to teach the Word to others. So committed was Ezra that his trip from Babylon to Jerusalem encompassed 900 miles over a four-month period.

Commitment comes in various degrees and levels. Are you committed like Ezra? If so, then your witness as an ambassador for Christ will be much stronger.

THE COACHES' CORNER

"All for One and One for All"

By Kathy Gray
Head Varsity Girl's Basketball Coach,
Valley Stream North H. S., NY

Commitment is one's obligation to dedicate time on a task fully and completely. Keeping this in mind, how do you get the high school athletes on your team to fully commit to the success of the entire team? That is a question that has plagued my program since I took over two years ago.

I coach a girl's basketball team that has not had a winning season in at least ten years. The girls on the team have been involved in track, kick line (dance), cheerleading, and soccer while playing basketball. There have been times when they have missed practice to go to another sport's event and sometimes they even will miss a game. Obviously, I am responsible for allowing this to occur, but I feel that my hands are tied.

The parents of the players allow them to make a commitment to two teams and expect it to be normal and acceptable for each commitment to be flexible. Commitment is not flexible. An athlete who does not show up for a practice or game because of another event is letting her teammates down. A team works hard on perfecting skills and plays and is only as strong as its weakest link. A person who is committed to a variety of events is taking away from the team's strength. The student-athlete who does not know the plays can ultimately be the difference between a win or a loss. But then this raises the commitment issue again. Those who are committed to many sports cannot take the time needed to learn the plays. They do not take time outside of the gym to learn what they have missed due to their involvement in other commitments. Their lack of knowledge regarding the plays demonstrates a lack of commitment.

Although I could mandate that the girls be allowed to play only one sport during the season so they are fully committed to that sport, I have been advised that a mandate of that nature would be unfair. However, I must disagree. In order to be successful, I believe your actions must exemplify your verbal commitment. You cannot say you're going to be a good team without first having a sincere, dedicated work ethic.

"Commitment Breeds Results"

By **Wylie Gober**
Freshman Boy's Basketball Coach,
Rice H. S., New York, NY

One of my many experiences in dealing with student-athletes occurred when I coached the freshman basketball team at Rice High School in Harlem, NY. The Rice Raiders are recognized as one of the premier basketball programs in the country. The Varsity A team travels to compete in some of the top tournaments nationwide.

Even though I am a laid-back, even-tempered individual by nature, I have been known to be tough on my players. I wanted them to give their best effort every time they stepped onto the court, taking no shortcuts. "Work hard or go home!" was my motto.

There was a situation in practice one day where I felt the team was not practicing hard. They were "going through the motions" and not giving their best effort. We had an important game coming up in a couple of days against one of our archrivals, Christ the King High School from Middle Village, NY. They had defeated us earlier in the season. Like most coaches, I am a fiery competitor and I hate to lose, and no one wants to lose to a team twice. I blew my whistle and told the team to line up on the baseline. They thought I was going to yell at them or make them run wind sprints. After a couple of minutes of silence, I finally told them, "We have practice tomorrow at 2:30 pm." I turned around and walked out the gym. I told the Junior Varsity coach he could have the gym because we were finished. They were stunned, because we had only practiced for about 15-20 minutes. As I sat in my office, the team went into the locker room laughing and fooling around. I was very upset and disappointed with their lack of effort and their attitudes. One of the players came into my office to see if I was all right. I told him I was fine, just tired. I told him to get home safely and to do his homework.

The next day before practice, I spoke to my assistant coach and told him I was going to try an old trick, the "be very demanding on your best player" tactic. I learned this psychological ploy from former NBA coaching great Hubie Brown at one of his clinics. My assistant told me it might be risky, but it was worth a try. The basic idea was to be hard on your best player in practice in order to create a positive, more energized and upbeat atmosphere. Thank God my best player and team captain had a quiet and low-key disposition. He did not react to us in a negative way. His energy, work ethic, and leadership skills permeated throughout the team and they followed suit. They were hustling, diving for loose balls, playing aggressive defense and an up tempo offense. The plan worked. We had one of our best practices of the season. We went out and beat the Christ the King team. It was a great learning experience for the young men and for me.

After the game, I spoke to them in the locker room about how important it was for them to come to practice and games completely focused and determined to give 110%. I told them you never know who may be watching. I reminded them an AAU coach or someone may approach me and ask about them and that they may be asked to play for another team during the off season. Therefore, it was important to carry themselves with dignity and respect. I also apologized to my best player for being overly demanding on him during practice. It helped bring the team closer together as a family. We went on to have a successful season, even though we lost in the championship game to Christ the King High School. The team learned valuable lessons in sportsmanship, dedication, teamwork, commitment, and life skills. Most of my players made and stayed on the Honor Roll and went on to play on the JV, Varsity A or B teams. I was very happy and proud of their maturation during their remaining years at Rice.

QUESTION AND ANSWER SESSION FEATURING:

Jason Harewood, Girl's Basketball – AAU Athletic Director, and The Scholar Athlete's **Eddie Grezensky**, Murray Bergtraum H. S.

Gerald Davis: How has a commitment for winning been instilled in your players?

Jason Harewood: That's a really tough question for me to answer because we focus more on giving your best effort and letting the outcome take care of itself. This is especially true with our younger athletes. However, with that being said, winning becomes more of an emphasis once the athlete enters high school. That's when we really stress the importance of achieving great success through winning. Usually in an AAU scenario it's paramount that you win, which invariably increases your opportunities to be seen by college coaches.

Typically during those college exposure tournaments, the last team standing is the one who had been able to maximize their exposure opportunities by virtue of the number of games they were able to play during the span of that event. That may not hold true all the time, but you're usually at a huge advantage if you made it to the final four. We try as much as possible to prepare the kids to be the best. That is always our goal – to compete at the highest level and not walk away from winning a big event or tournament.

Eddie Grezensky: A commitment to winning has to be established from day one. It starts with your work ethic in practice and carries over into your games.

Gerald Davis: When players don't exhibit the same commitment level you have, how does that make you feel?

Jason Harewood: We're sort of going through that right now, and I can tell you it is very frustrating, to say the least. I have a young team, only half of which are committed to excelling and getting better. As much as I have tried to find the right buttons to push, I have finally had to resolve myself to the fact that some players just don't want it to the extent that their coaches and in many cases their parents would like to see them achieve.

Sometimes you can accept things the way they are, or, as in my case, tear it down and build it all over again. That's sort if where we are right now with this most recent team. We will try our best to keep those players who are truly committed and weed out those who don't want to put forth the necessary level of effort and commitment. I'm of the philosophy that it takes several years to build a championship team or program. The pruning is a necessary process that nature requires for growth and improvement.

Not every player will exhibit the same commitment that you have. However, your core players must have this level of commitment if you are to be a championship team.

Gerald Davis: How do you go about changing that mindset, or can you?

Jason Harewood: We always take to showing them the big picture in hopes that it will one day click in their minds and they'll realize, *I really can have some measure of success in this game.* Sometimes it is just a matter of them actually experiencing that success, which invariably creates a new level of excitement about what it is they are trying to achieve. I remember one year while competing for an AAU National championship we had the fortunate opportunity of meeting a few of the Duke Women's basketball players. Well, that was all we needed to do to inspire one of our players to push herself to one day wear a Duke uniform. Sure enough, she's wearing one now, and I would have to believe that very brief encounter with those Duke players helped push this young lady to another level of commitment towards preparing herself to become one of the best in her class.

Eddie Grezensky: Pressure from your core players is the best way to change the mindset of an unmotivated player. Sometimes it becomes necessary to remove a player from the team who does not go along with the program.

3-POINTERS

Matthew 10:38 (KJV) – *And he that taketh not his cross, and followeth after me, is not worthy of me.*

Luke 9:23-24 (KJV) – *And he said to them all, if any man will come after me, let him deny himself, and take up his cross daily, and follow me. For whosoever will save his life shall lose it: but whosoever will lose his life for my sake, the same shall save it.*

Psalm 37:4-5 (KJV) – *Delight thyself also in the Lord; and he shall give thee the desires of thine heart. Commit thy way unto the Lord; trust also in him; and he shall bring it to pass.*

BUZZER BEATER

If you wish for success in life, make perseverance your bosom friend.

- Joseph Addison

POST-GAME NOTES

....
....
....
....
....
....
....

DIGNITY ... *Proud and self-respecting character*

Read: Mark 16:9-11

Key Verse: 1 Samuel 16:7 – *But the Lord said to Samuel, "Don't judge by a man's face or height, for this is not the one. I don't make decisions the way you do! Men judge by outward appearance, but I look at a man's thoughts and intentions."*

Show me a coach that doesn't get angry or upset and I'll show you a person who may be void of emotions. Because of the competitive nature of sports, it's close to borderline impossible not to have some degree of anger at times, whether that anger is displayed towards a referee, umpire, a player, a fan, or parent. It's a certainty that anger will arrive in one form or another. It can be displayed by a particular look, a sudden shout of displeasure or even in one's body language. It will happen; I guarantee it! However, it still doesn't permit the Christian to bring shame to himself, his faith, or to God. While I understand it's difficult to refrain from showing any form of anger at all, one must use some level of civility when those occasions arise. If you've ever been on the receiving end of a tongue-lashing, you know how bad it makes you feel, not to mention how much it destroys your self-esteem. No one wants to be berated. Being a coach doesn't give you the freedom to degrade someone whenever you feel the need to do so, especially when it comes to correcting a player during a game or practice. As a coach, I understand that screaming sometimes erupts from your lips before you have a chance to stop it – I don't deny it. But keep in mind that someone is always watching. With that being said, don't even think of crossing the line and adding cursing to the mix. It will usually make a bad situation worse. Besides, cursing is a sign of an unclean spirit and a limited vocabulary.

Mary Magdalene lived in a time when woman were treated like second-class citizens. Women were often on the receiving end of many angry outbursts. The saying "being seen and not heard" didn't just pertain to children, but to women also. Regardless of one's sex one wants to be treated with respect. Jesus treated everyone the same. No gender was believed to be better than the other, with each receiving love and dignity in abundance. Mary received this firsthand from Jesus because she was an ardent follower of Christ. During many of Christ's travels with His disciples, Mary was usually right there among them learning from Jesus as well. What she saw on a daily basis was Christ treating all human beings with dignity and respect.

THE COACHES' CORNER

QUESTION AND ANSWER SESSION FEATURING:

Gordon Miles, High School Basketball Official, New York, NY

Gerald Davis: The job of being a basketball official comes with a great deal of responsibility. How do you believe officials should conduct themselves on the court during times of disagreement with players or coaches?

Gordon Miles: I believe officials should conduct themselves with respect and honor. Officials are given a position of power. The responsibility of an official should include having a high level of self-esteem and poise. A good official always uses three key elements to make accurate and fair decisions; these are time, thoughts, and actions:

- Time to think about the disagreement
- Thoughts that will direct your actions
- Actions to make your time, thoughts, and decisions meaningful

3-POINTERS

Romans 12:3 (KJV) – For I say, through the grace given unto me, to every man that is among you, not to think of himself more highly than he ought to think; but to think soberly, according as God hath dealt to every man the measure of faith.

Psalm 31:23 (KJV) – O love the Lord, all ye his saints: for the Lord preserveth the faithful, and plentifully rewardeth the proud doer.

Psalm 84:11 (KJV) – *The Lord bestows favor and honor; no good thing does He withhold from those whose walk is blameless.*

BUZZER BEATER

Self-command is the main elegance.

- Ralph Waldo Emerson

POST-GAME NOTES

....
....
....
....
....
....
....

DISCIPLINE ... *a trained condition of order and obedience*

Read: 1 Samuel 2:12-26

Key Verse: 1 Samuel 2:17 (KJV) – *Wherefore the sin of the young men was very great before the LORD: for men abhorred the offering of the LORD.*

Regardless of the personality type of a coach, there will be occasions during the course of a season when a coach will have to discipline a player or even a staff member – and if you haven't yet faced this uncomfortable task as a coach, your time is coming. When discipline *is* necessary, how will you handle the situation? The answer usually lies within the personality of the individual or the situation. Are you a screamer or the "calm, cool, collected" type? Do you keep your frustrations and anger bottled up on the inside, and then once it begins to boil over you finally dispense discipline? Or do you handle problem situations right there on the spot when they occur? Whatever the answer, it's important that the essence of your message is conveyed and adhered to. Remember, it's the coach who is ultimately responsible for the good order of the program, whether the situation that disrupts this order presents itself on or off the court. How you handle difficult situations is a reflection of you as a leader. You certainly wouldn't want someone embarrassing you or your institution.

In the Old Testament we learn of how those embarrassing moments were taken to new heights by Eli's sons, Hophni and Phinehas. Eli was a high priest and a judge of Israel who could not control his sons. To put it mildly, his sons were "head cases". They didn't respect their father or his position as worship leader. They didn't respect the temple or even God Almighty Himself. They made a normal practice of taking for themselves parts of sacrifices that hadn't yet been offered to God. They also seduced young women in the tabernacle. Now these were very serious offenses. It got to the point where God's mercy was taken to the limit, so much so that He wanted them both killed because of their disobedience. God held Eli responsible for his failure to discipline his children. Eli didn't speak to them about their behavior, and God knew that Eli hadn't taken decisive action, either. Actions (or sometimes the lack thereof, as in this case) speak louder than words.

Because of the seriousness of Eli's disobedience, the discipline issue could not be overlooked. In the Old Testament, the responsibility of the high priest was to serve as a mediator – he represented God to the people and the people to God. The high priest who conducted those sacrifices had to live a life of holiness. If he didn't, the spirit of God killed the high priest while he was in the courts of the Holy of Holies. A priest had to exemplify the sinless character of God himself. Thankfully, Jesus Christ was chosen to be our high priest forever. Christ now sits on the right-hand side of the Father, interceding for us.

THE COACHES' CORNER

QUESTION AND ANSWER SESSION FEATURING:

Thomas Schiavo, Head Football Coach at Valley Stream North H. S., Valley Stream, NY

Gerald Davis: Do you consider yourself to be a disciplinarian as a football coach?

Thomas Schiavo: Am I a disciplinarian? Well, sometimes, when necessary. I try to lay down the rules, only four, and policies, about a dozen, and let things run themselves from there. If I have to, I will be very stern with my players. I have a program called "The Sponsor Program" that I use when a student athlete gets out of line. It's pretty simple: another player has to take responsibility for the penalty portion of the player who is screwing up. It's based on peer pressure, something a player can put on another player that a coach can't. I got the idea from my friend Jim Bernhardt (the running backs' coach at UCF). I'm blessed with good kids most of the time, and discipline really isn't an issue. Now that we are becoming a better program, competition for positions makes kids behave better simply because behavioral issues will also determine if a kid plays or doesn't play.

Gerald Davis: Why is discipline important in your program?

Thomas Schiavo: Discipline is important for many reasons. I believe that if you can't rely on a kid to be disciplined in the classroom or in the hallways, you can't reply on him to be disciplined on game day. Consistently displaying self-discipline is one way a kid shows me that he is ready, willing, and able to play.

Gerald Davis: Do you believe today's players prefer disciplinarians as coaches?

Thomas Schiavo: Some do and some don't. It depends on the kid … it depends on the kid's family. It also depends on the programs the kid participates in. Do they have self-discipline, or are they chaotic? Some thrive in a disciplined environment and some crumble.

Gerald Davis: Can a program exist without discipline?

Thomas Schiavo: Yes, a program can exist without discipline. It may crash and burn in an instant, but it can exist for a short period of time. However, I don't believe that a program can **thrive** without discipline. Kids are kids, and as such they need the structure that a disciplined environment provides. There needs to be some sort of rules and expectations, and then consequences for breaking those rules. However, I've found that the fewer the rules, the better. Our four rules are: 1) be on time; 2) be prepared; 3) participate; 4) the "do right" rule (meaning, use appropriate language, don't steal, respect team members and equipment, and so on).

3-POINTERS

Proverbs 3:11-12 (NASB) – *My son, do not reject the discipline of the Lord, or loathe his reproof, for whom the Lord loves he reproves, even as a father, the son in whom he delights.*

Proverbs 29:15 (NASB) – *The rod and reproof give wisdom, but a child who gets his own way brings shame to his mother.*

Ephesians 6:4 (NASB) – *And, fathers, do not provoke your children to anger; but bring them up in the discipline and instruction of the Lord.*

BUZZER BEATER

Self-control is the quality that distinguishes the fittest to survive.

- George Bernard Shaw

POST-GAME NOTES

....

....

....

....

....

....

....

GRACIOUS ... *pleasant, kindly, courteous*

Read: Genesis 37:1-36

Key Verse: Genesis 37:5 – *One night Joseph had a dream, and promptly reported the details to his brothers, causing even deeper hatred.*

Is there anything worse than a sore loser? I think there is – it's called an ungracious winner. Everyone who plays or coaches a game does so with the intention and desire of winning. Herman Edwards, the former head coach of the New York Jets, put it this way: "You play to win the game." He is absolutely right, but after the final horn or whistle is blown, everyone involved should conduct themselves with class and dignity, including you as the coach whether your team came away with a win or a loss.

A coach that I have always admired is Coach Mike Krzyzweski of Duke University, not just for his championships or his 700-plus wins, but also for how he carries himself *after* a win or a loss. Some might say that a coach who has 700 wins doesn't have enough practice in losing. That's not entirely true, because along with those wins came some heart-breaking defeats. During some of those defeats that I have witnessed, he has always conducted himself graciously: from a congratulatory handshake with the opposing coaches and players, to complimentary quotes in the newspaper regarding his opponent's performance.

The Old Testament story of Joseph details that at the young age of seventeen he was a "tad-bit" smug, overbearing, and conceited. Joseph knew that he was the favorite child of his father Jacob. He wasn't too shy in expressing this fact to his ten brothers, either. His cocky attitude quickly made him an outcast. When he wasn't showing off his brightly colored coat that was given to him by his father, he was interpreting his God-given dreams in a way that could not be considered gracious. Let's take a look at those dreams and Joseph's interpretations of them, which he freely shared with his brothers:

Dream # 1: "We were out in the fields binding sheaves and my sheaf stood up and your sheaves all gathered around it and bowed low before it!"

Dream # 2: "The sun, moon, and eleven stars bowed low before me!"

It is true that these dreams *did* speak about how one day Joseph would become a leader and his brothers would be his subordinates. While it's great to be excited about the good things that God is doing and revealing in your life, God doesn't want you to be a braggart.

Joseph's dreams proved to be prophetic over time. Also with time, his maturity grew.

Joseph learned how to be gracious.

THE COACHES' CORNER

QUESTION AND ANSWER SESSION FEATURING:

Thomas Schiavo, Head Football Coach at Valley Stream North H. S., Valley Stream, NY

Gerald Davis: Can sportsmanship and aggressiveness go hand-in-hand?

Thomas Schiavo: Good players need to be aggressive, and great players **must** be aggressive! You can be extremely aggressive and still display good sportsmanship. Play between the whistles and obey the rules. Play hard. When you hustle all the way across the field to tackle someone, get there with a sense of purpose. You can help them up after the tackle if you choose to do so. The whistle is like an ON/OFF switch. Control your emotions. If you're not super-aggressive, you will not respect yourself as a player and even worse, your opponent won't respect you either. Being aggressive doesn't mean that you are unsportsmanlike.

3-POINTERS

Ephesians 1:8 (LB) – And he has showered down upon us the richness of his grace – for how well he understand us and knows what is best for us at all times.

1 Peter 3:8 (KJV) – Finally, be ye all of one mind, having compassion one of another, love as brethren, be pitiful, be courteous.

2 Peter 1:7 (KJV) – And to godliness brotherly kindness; and to brotherly kindness charity.

BUZZER BEATER

A man wrapped up in himself makes a very small bundle.
- Benjamin Franklin

POST-GAME NOTES

....
....
....
....
....
....
....

INTEGRITY ... *honesty; sincerity; uprightness*

Read: Matthew 1:18-25

Key Verses: Matthew 1:23-24 – *Listen! The virgin shall conceive a child! She shall give birth to a son, and he shall be called "Emmanuel" when Joseph awoke, he did as the angel commanded, and brought Mary home to be his wife.*

Motion picture director Spike Lee (and number-one Knicks fan) must have gotten his inspiration for his film title "Do the Right Thing" from Joseph. Joseph was Jesus Christ's earthly father; he was chosen because he was a man of integrity. Mary, Jesus' mother, was Joseph's fiancée. It was the Holy Spirit who impregnated Mary with the child who would be called Jesus – the King of kings and the Savior of the world. This put both Mary and Joseph in a precarious situation. First, Mary was in an obvious state of being with child without being married. Joseph stayed with a woman who was pregnant without the benefits of a husband/wife intimacy. It was the foreknowledge of God that prepared Joseph's heart. However, it still took faith, courage, and obedience for Joseph to follow through with the original plans of matrimony. Joseph, however, wasn't your ordinary man. He was a man's man – a man of conviction and integrity whose words equaled his actions.

The integrity of a man is not measured by what he says but by what he does when conflicts, challenges, and awkward situations arise. If you were Joseph, how would you have handled the situation? Would you have stayed committed to Mary or would you have escaped on the first mule out of town? Thankfully, Joseph was a man of integrity who would be just the right earthly father for Jesus.

Integrity involves having the inner fortitude of Christ. Integrity is doing the right thing when everyone else is following the crowd. I'm sure you've heard it said before by a friend or family member: "Well, so-and-so did it or does it." But isn't that just like the world and human nature, where the majority wants to make doing that which is unrighteous acceptable? Problems arise when shortcuts are taken and when truth is only in operation if and when it's convenient. It is my belief that every parent or guardian wants a man or woman of integrity coaching their son or daughter. Be that person of integrity!

THE COACHES' CORNER

QUESTION AND ANSWER SESSION FEATURING:

Robert Dinardo, Head Women's Basketball Coach at Concordia College, NY

Gerald Davis: In today's game cheating is so commonplace. How have you been able to stay aboveboard in your recruiting practices?

Robert Dinardo: For me it has always been easy to be an honest coach and *not* cheat. Cheating is a betrayal of everything a coach is supposed to stand for. A coach is also an educator first, and no good educator cheats. If you run an honest program, everyone benefits in the long run.

3-POINTERS

Psalm 119:1-3 (NASB) – *How blessed are those whose way is blameless, who walk in the law of the Lord. How blessed are those who observe his testimonies, who seek Him with all their heart. They also do no unrighteousness; they walk in his ways.*

Psalm 92:12-13 (NIV) – *The righteous man will flourish like the palm tree, they will grow like a cedar of Lebanon; planted in the house of the Lord, they will flourish in the courts of our God.*

Psalm 112:1 (KJV) – *Praise ye the Lord. Blessed is the man that feareth the Lord, that delighteth greatly in his commandments.*

BUZZER BEATER

Decisions are not made at a particular moment of time; they are rooted in a man's character.

- A. R. Bernard

POST-GAME NOTES

....
....
....
....
....
....
....

LEADERSHIP ... *the position, function, or guidance of a leader*

Read: Joshua 1:1-17

Key Verses: Joshua 1:17-18 – *"We will obey you just as we obeyed Moses," they assured him, "and may the Lord your God be with you as he was with Moses. If anyone, no matter who, rebels against your commands, he shall die. So lead on with courage and strength!"*

There are many different ways to lead. Some coaches delegate authority. Some are very vocal and outspoken and some do it quietly. Regardless of how one leads, there are certain qualities that should always remain on the inside. Are you fearless? Are you intelligent? Most importantly, are you respected?

When you're respected as a leader, your players will go the extra mile and dig a little deeper to find the best within themselves. Even when there are two minutes on the clock and you're down by twenty, your team will rally behind you! This type of respect is not given; it's earned.

When the coach exemplifies these character traits on a daily basis, it goes a long way in establishing a level of trust between that coach and his/her players, and therefore it becomes much easier to lead them. Your players can only duplicate the effort they see you putting forth.

As a leader, you are always in a position where you can be "second guessed." That is why as a coach I want to be as well prepared as I possibly can be. However, that is not my only desire. It's my hope that I consistently walk in the will of God, my heavenly Father.

Joshua in the Old Testament was a military strategist and a personal assistant to Moses for forty years. Joshua would also eventually welcome the spirit of God in his life. Joshua witnessed firsthand how the children of Israel were a "stiff-necked" people. They questioned almost everything; they even criticized their blessings. Joshua understood something that every Christian leader must realize – that we cannot go through any situation without God's help or His presence in the situation with us. If we think we can, we are sorely mistaken. As a coach you want to be sensitive to the leading of the spirit of God. When God speaks, you listen! Joshua was able to navigate through many challenges because of this belief.

THE COACHES' CORNER

"Are You A Leader?"

By **Brad Oringer**, Assistant Men's Basketball Coach, The City College of New York, NY

Leadership is one factor every coach talks about. There isn't just one definition for it, but you can recognize fairly quickly a player who has leadership qualities.

In 2003, the basketball program at CCNY was blessed with two great senior leaders, Dana Warner and Edwin Caceres. You had to be around the team on a daily basis to see the impact these two had on it. Let me just say that any coach at any program wishes he had leaders like them.

Dana and Eddie faced a challenging task. They were the only seniors on the team. The other six kids who played significantly were freshmen and sophomores. This is why leadership is not only on the court. I could see the impact they had in the locker room, weight room, study hall, cafeteria, and on the bus trips. They took charge from day one.

We ended up winning the conference title with 17 wins but it wasn't a smooth ride. At one point we had a 5 – 9 record, and with so many young guys the season could've been over. However, Dana and Eddie wouldn't allow it. They knew that both the coaches and the younger players really needed them. This was the classic case of two guys merely saying, "Follow us," and everyone did because they knew the kind of young men Dana and Eddie were. They led by example and set the tone and direction for the rest of the season.

I'm sure we as coaches at CCNY might be a bit spoiled after having had Dana and Eddie for one year. It takes a while to realize not everyone is up to the challenge of leadership. The most telling statement came recently from a returning junior who said, "I'm not into leading anyone anywhere."

QUESTION AND ANSWER SESSION FEATURING:

Minister **Hosea James Givan II**, Educator
I Love Our Youth, Inc., Queens, NY

Gerald Davis: What makes a good leader?
Hosea James Givan II: The best leaders lead by example. This is not always in what they say, but what they do! A good leader should be able to communicate well and be able to effectively express his or her thoughts. A good leader should be trustworthy as well as capable of establishing the trust of those who follow him or her. Being able to take risks and having good listening skills are the final two attributes I would list of what makes a good leader.

Gerald Davis: Who are some leaders that you admire from the sports community and why?
Hosea James Givan II: There are four who come to mind almost immediately: 1) Magic Johnson – He's the epitome of unselfishness;

2) Mariano Rivera – a true professional; 3) Derek Jeter – He's a quiet man, but he leads by example; 4) Coach Mike Krzyzewski – He's a great motivator.

3-POINTERS

1 Thessalonians 5:12-13 (NASB) – *But we request of you, brethren, that you appreciate those who diligently labor among you, and have charge over you in the Lord and give you instruction and that you esteem them very highly in love because of their work. Live in peace with one another.*

1 Timothy 1:7 (KJV) – *For God hath not given us the spirit of fear but of power, and of love, and of a sound mind.*

Proverbs 22:6 (HCS) – *Teach a youth about the way he should go; even when he is old he will not depart from it.*

BUZZER BEATER

You become a leader when you decide not to be a copy but an original.

- Dr. Myles Munroe

POST-GAME NOTES

....
....
....
....
....
....
....

LOYALTY ... *being true and faithful to love, promise, duty, or other obligations*

Read: 1 Samuel 26:1-25

Key Verse: 1 Samuel 26:25 – *And Saul said to David, "Blessings on you, my son David. You shall do heroic deeds and be a great conqueror."*

Battles! I laugh in the face of them. Secret Missions! Bring them on! Abi shai, one of King David's soldiers, often displayed this fearlessness without consequence (sometimes to a fault). While his reasoning skills often came into question, no one doubted his loyalty. He was someone you could count on.

My wish for every head coach is to have assistant coaches he or she can count on. To be successful in the coaching business, you need dedicated and loyal assistants. Having their help can also lessen the workload, which can enable the coach to concentrate on coaching, teaching, and refining the details in the program.

In many programs, the assistant is the "Jack of all trades." He's the recruiter, travel coordinator, bus driver, and den mother; mediator, liaison, psychologist, and practice player. The good assistant will relish the learning opportunities and do them well, because, in most cases, the assistant has his own career aspirations of being a head coach. With this in mind, he must believe and understand that faithful service will not go unrewarded or unnoticed. Someone is always watching; most importantly, your Heavenly Father is.

THE COACHES' CORNER

"Loyalty Is a Two-way Street"

By **Deirdre Moore**, Assistant Women's Basketball Coach, C. W. Post University, Long Island, NY

As a coach, you always want your players to be loyal to you. I feel, however, that there are not enough coaches who are loyal to their players. This is something that is really disturbing to me. Why do so many coaches feel they are "better" or "too good?" Why is it okay for coaches not to support their players? Being loyal means being faithful to a person.

Players feel so many times that their coaches have given up on them. For example, I have seen coaches take players' scholarships. Where is the loyalty? You have recruited this athlete. They try hard, practice hard, and still have difficulty producing. The coach needs to take responsibility for this. Maybe your assessment of this player's skill level or potential was incorrect. Yet some coaches will find a way to remove this player from the roster. I believe that if you do the right thing, the right thing will come back to you. The reverse is also true. If you do the wrong thing, bad things will come back to you. Coaches need to be loyal to their players. I've coached a player whose skill level may not have been up to par with the other players on the team, yet I was able to get great production out of her. She knew that I was loyal to her. She didn't feel that I was overlooking her or not coaching her. In turn, she produced good results. In some cases she produced better than players with more talent. If you want loyalty, you must be loyal.

QUESTION AND ANSWER SESSION FEATURING:

Joe Gugliero, Women's and Girl's Basketball Coach, Long Island, NY

Gerald Davis: What does loyalty mean to you?

Joe Gugliero: We can do nothing of significance on our own. Human life, at the most fundamental level, cannot be sustained without cooperative effort, and cooperative effort is impossible without loyalty. Loyalty allows the talent and the will of individuals to be directed towards a common goal, whether that goal is survival itself or the simple task of winning a basketball game.

Gerald Davis: On a scale of 1 to 10, where would you rank loyalty when hiring an assistant coach? Please explain.

Joe Gugliero: 10! The chemistry and emotional stability of a team is extremely delicate and is prone to the subtlest shifts of the wind. One of the things that makes coaching at the college level so challenging is the fact that your success depends largely on your ability to pull kids together in the face of their conflicting interests, diverging personalities, and incompatible sets of values. The fact that the coach is trying to accomplish this with post-adolescent kids who are just beginning to sprout wings and come to grips with who they really are as people adds enormously to this already challenging task. A really good coaching staff is able to establish a culture that supersedes all the factors that tend to pull teams apart. The coaches set the standards, establish the rules, and dole out the rewards and punishment. If the kids do not respect the coaching staff, they will not subdue their individual interests for the good of the team.

When that happens, you have no team – instead you have anarchy! If coaches want to truly lead kids, they must walk the walk as well as talk the talk. A coaching staff that preaches honesty and loyalty but quarrels in front of kids and talks disparagingly behind each other's backs is doomed to fail. The kids see everything!

An assistant coach who is not loyal to the head coach can single-handedly bring a program to its knees.

3-POINTERS

Romans 13:1 (NASB) – Let every person be in subjection to the governing authorities. For there is no authority except from God, and those which exist are established by God.

Titus 3:1 (NASB) – Remind them to be subject to rulers, to authorities, to be obedient, to be ready for every good deed.

Deuteronomy 7:9 (NASB) – Know therefore that the Lord your God, He is God, the faithful God, who keeps his covenant and his loving kindness to a thousandth generation with those who love him and keep his commandments.

BUZZER BEATER

The only way to have a friend is to be one.

- Ralph Waldo Emerson

POST-GAME NOTES

....
....
....
....
....
....
....

OBEDIENCE ... *doing what one is told; submission to authority or law*

Read: Genesis 4:1-15

Key Verse: Hebrews 11:4 – *It was by faith that Abel obeyed God and brought an offering that pleased God more than Cain's offering did. God accepted Abel and proved it by accepting his gift; and though Abel is long dead, we can still learn lessons from him about trusting God.*

Playing basketball has been likened to performing a ballet on hardwood. However, it is not always about running up and down the court, playing racehorse basketball. The athleticism of basketball players is breathtaking. The jumping ability and quickness displayed is not like any other sport. But there will be times in a game when the pace is slow and set plays must be executed. When those times come, you want to see the results of your hard work. There is a difference between ad-libbing an offensive set when a play breaks down and when a point guard or any other positioned player is openly defiant and disobedient. When the latter occurs, you must take action. The seeds of disobedience cannot be given a chance to grow among your team members.

God gave both Cain and Abel specific instructions on how to prepare a sacrifice. While the farmer Cain's offering was rejected, the shepherd Abel's was accepted. The Bible doesn't go into an explanation of why Cain's offering was unacceptable, but the key point that is made is that both brothers understood what had to be produced (verse 6). The end results were clear: one brother chose to obey God and one chose to disobey.

THE COACHES' CORNER

QUESTION AND ANSWER SESSION FEATURING:

Brenda Morgan, Head Varsity Girl's Basketball Coach, Abraham Lincoln H. S., Brooklyn, NY

… and…

Andy Stampfel, Head Men's Basketball Coach, The City College of New York, NY, NY

Gerald Davis: What are some of the team rules you have in place?

Brenda Morgan: The first and foremost team rule we have is that the players must demonstrate respect for themselves, their coaches, and their teammates. They are informed at the first meeting that they are "student" athletes. The emphasis is on their being a "student" first and then an athlete. Our most important concern is for a student to have passing grades while respecting the staff and his or her fellow students. During a game they are absolutely forbidden to approach a referee. If that happens they're automatically sat down. Disrespect is totally unacceptable and they know it. One rule that really gets some of them upset is that regardless of who hits the floor, whether it's a teammate or someone from the opposing team, someone better be over to extend a hand to help them up. There is too much animosity in the game (that's my only criticism). It really upsets me to see how some of the coaches condone that type of behavior, and some even encourage it.

Last but not least, we teach our athletes to "respect all but fear none." We prepare our team to compete with the confidence that they can beat any team on any given day. "For one man's disobedience many were made sinners, so by the obedience of one many shall be made righteous."

Gerald Davis: Andy, what are some of the team rules you have in place?

Andy Stampfel: We have three team rules. One, be early! If you are not early, you're late. And that is for everything. Two, go to every class. Third, have a great positive attitude in everything you do and with everyone you interact with. We try to teach the kids to have a great attitude in attacking the weights, in getting better every day in practice, but especially to have a great attitude with teammates, teachers, and administrators.

Gerald Davis: Depending on the offense, how is a player reprimanded for any **egregious** behavior?

Brenda Morgan: Depending on the offense of a player, when a player does something totally out of this universe, the natural thing to do is ask, "What was **that**?!" We normally run a motion offense with many different options, so that gives them an out. And, if it's blatant disobedience, they have earned themselves a seat on the bench. Then we watch the film and they have some explaining to do with the entire team present. They know there are consequences for disobedience. However, I am against using exercise as discipline. Exercise should never be used as punishment. It's the norm for these girls to just forget the play during a game, whether it's due to nerves or inexperience. Some of them just freeze; it's part of the learning process.

Andy Stampfel: Whenever someone tries to go off on their own and do whatever they want to do while getting away from the "team," they are first given a verbal warning. If they don't get it together but instead just continue to play selfish basketball, then I pull them out and sit them on the bench. I'll explain to them what is going on and why it's not what we want. Usually this happens when players get frustrated, if they are having a bad night, or if they feel they haven't touched the ball for a while. This past season, as a matter of fact, we had the MVP of the league on our team. But the kid never passed the ball, never ran a play or the offense. He lasted the first three games of the season, and then I had to let him go for more reasons than that. He was not a team player and caused too much of a distraction.

3-POINTERS

Luke 11:28 (NIV) – He replied, "Blessed rather are those who hear the word of God and obey it.

John 15:10 (NIV) – If you obey my commands, you will remain in my love, just as I have obeyed my father's commands and remain in his love.

1 Samuel 15:22 (NIV) – To obey is better than sacrifice.

BUZZER BEATER

An ounce of obedience is worth more than a ton of prayer.
-Edwin Louis Cole

POST-GAME NOTES

....
....
....
....
....
....
....

STUDENT ... *one who studies; an attentive and systematic observer*

Read: Acts 18:23-28

Key Verses: Acts 18:25-26 – *While he was in Egypt, someone had told him about John the Baptist and what John had said about Jesus, but that is all he knew. He had never heard the rest of the story! So he was preaching boldly and enthusiastically in the synagogue, "The Messiah is coming! Get ready to receive him!" "Pricilla and Aquila were there and heard him – and it was a powerful sermon. Afterwards they met him and explained what had happened to Jesus since the time of John, and all that it meant!*

The good coaches are the ones who tell you they are not afraid to utilize ideas from other coaches or programs that have been successful– and then integrate those within their own beliefs or philosophy as a coach.

If you want to be a good coach, your ego must be non-existent. Coaching is like any other profession; you never stop learning. There are many different avenues of learning that you can take. You can learn from other coaches through basketball clinics and lectures. Books, tapes, and sports television programs can also be key in the learning process. Lessons can also be drawn from the very players you are coaching. Learning is a never-ending adventure.

In the New Testament, Apollos was a gifted and talented speaker. He preached throughout the region of Ephesus and did so effectively. However, while his enthusiasm for teaching the Word was at a maximum level, his knowledge of scripture wasn't always complete. His messages were taken from the Old Testament and John the Baptist – whereas Jesus' death and resurrection should have been at the forefront of what he preached. Apollos possessed the spirit of a disciple (a learner). If arrogance had been part of his personality, he would not have taken constructive criticism **or** learned the complete message of the Gospel, which was taught to him by Priscilla and Aquila.

THE COACHES' CORNER

QUESTION AND ANSWER SESSION FEATURING:

Paul Nixon, Head Women's Basketball Coach, Columbia University, NY

Gerald Davis: Please detail something new that you have learned during the course of the basketball season that you didn't know prior to the beginning of the season.

Paul Nixon: Prior to the beginning of this season I had never been a head coach before. After twelve years as an assistant coach, following four years as a student assistant in college, I believed I was ready. What I learned during the course of my first season is that I was prepared for the basketball side of things, meaning, I was ready to coach in games. What I did not know was how much goes into being a head coach that has nothing to do directly with winning or losing games. The administrative side of the position really took me by surprise because I thought I was ready for that, but experience has taught me some valuable lessons in how to be a more organized leader.

Gerald Davis: Who has been the most thought provoking speaker you have heard on the topic of basketball?

Paul Nixon: The most thought provoking speaker I have heard on the topic of basketball has been Van Chancellor. He is the head coach and general manager for the 4-time champion Houston Comets of the WNBA, and he was the USA Basketball head coach for the women's team that won gold medals in the 2002 World Championships in China and the 2004 Summer Olympic Games in Athens, Greece. He is a very entertaining speaker, but he is also very knowledgeable of the game. He speaks about the game of basketball from a perspective I can definitely relate to.

He is also a strong Christian family man who I believe serves as a great role model for young male coaches.

3-POINTERS

Proverbs 1:5 (NASB) – *A wise man will hear and increase in learning, and a man of understanding will acquire wise counsel.*

Proverbs 8:10-11 (NASB) – *Take my instruction, and not silver, and knowledge rather than choicest gold. For wisdom is better than jewels; and all desirable things cannot compare with her.*

Proverbs 8:33 (KJV) – *Hear instruction, and be wise, and refuse it not.*

BUZZER BEATER

The smartest thing I ever said was, "Help me!"

- Anonymous

POST-GAME NOTES

....
....
....
....
....
....
....

TRAILBLAZER ... *a person who pioneers or prepares the way for something new*

Read: John 1:19-34

Key Verses: John 1:29-30 – *The next day John saw Jesus coming toward him and said, "Look! There is the Lamb of God who takes away the world's sin! He is the one I was talking about when I* *said, 'Soon a man far greater than I am is coming, who existed long before me!'"*

A trailblazer is someone who prepares the way or path for someone else. It's usually the kind of person who doesn't mind taking risks. A trailblazer is innovative, fearless, and creative. John the Baptist was just such an individual. His desire, determination, and **due-diligence** in foretelling the coming of the true Messiah were revolutionary. His exploits are well documented in the four Gospels of the New Testament. Being bold and proclaiming truth was what made John the man of God he was. His bravery may have also contributed to his death. Some may consider what John did as dangerous. Even so, that is what a trailblazer is – the ultimate risk-taker!

If I were to give examples of all the trailblazing minds in the game of basketball, the list of names would be too long to mention, but here are some who particularly stand out:

Bobby Knight – the motion offense
Pete Carril – the Princeton Offense
Pete Newell – the Low Post Play
John Wooden – for his ON/OFF court philosophy
John Chaney – Match-up Zone Defense
Tex Winter – the Triangle Offense
Jerry Tarkanian – the Amoeba Defense
Pat Summitt – Tennessee Basketball
Tara Vanderveer – The Stanford System

Each one in his or her own right has been an innovative trailblazer. These are coaches who have not been afraid to put their own spin on existing sets of defenses and offenses. The key factor for the success of these men and women was their fearlessness in the face of failure. Like John the Baptist, they were not afraid of new beginnings and facing the challenge of paving new roads.

It takes these types of coaches for all sports programs to grow. How else can we expand and experience the fullness and expressive nature that God has given us? Therefore, I challenge you to start trailblazing so that others will follow in your footsteps and in time, hopefully inspire others to become leaders and trailblazers themselves as well.

THE COACHES' CORNER

QUESTION AND ANSWER SESSION FEATURING:

Brad Oringer, Assistant Men's Basketball Coach, The City College of New York, NY, NY

Gerald Davis: Coaches are known for copying, especially if what is being copied is working successfully for another coach. Which trailblazing coaching techniques have produced positive results for you, even if you may have questioned them at first?

Brad Oringer: Concepts like Rick Pitino's match-up press is excellent. We would love to utilize it in our system. However, our players have not been able to make it work.

Gerald Davis: What contribution would you like to be known for among the basketball community?

Brad Oringer: I'd love for my main contribution to be kids coming back to visit us years from now saying our coaches, school, and team made a difference in their lives.

3-POINTERS

Genesis 41:15 (NASB) – Pharaoh said, Joseph, "I have had a dream, but no one can interpret it; and I have heard it said about you, that when you hear a dream you can interpret it."

Numbers 27:15-18 (NASB) – Then Moses spoke to the Lord, saying, "May the Lord, the God of the spirits of all flesh, appoint a man over the congregation, who will go out and come in before them, and who will lead them out and bring them in, that the congregation of the Lord may not be like sheep which have no shepherd." So the Lord said to Moses,

"Take Joshua the son of Nun, a man in whom is the spirit, and lay your hand on him."

1 Chronicles 22:7-10 (NASB) – *And David said to Solomon, "My son, I had intended to build a house to the name of the Lord my God. But the word of the Lord came to me, saying, 'You have shed much blood, and have waged great wars; you shall not build a house to my name, because you have shed so much blood on the earth before me. Behold, a son shall be born to you, who shall be a man of rest; and I will give rest from all his enemies on every side; for his name shall be Solomon, and I will give peace and quiet to Israel in his days. He shall build a house for my name, and he shall be my son, and I will be his father; and I will establish the throne of his kingdom over Israel forever.'"*

BUZZER BEATER

Think you can, think you can't, either way, you'll be right.

- Henry Ford

POST-GAME NOTES

....
....
....
....
....
....
....

UPSETS ... *to gain an unexpected victory*

Read: 1 Samuel 17:1-58

Key Verse: 1 Samuel 17:48-49 – *As Goliath moved closer to attack, David quickly ran out to meet him. Reaching into his shep-*

herd's bag and taking out a stone, he hurled it with his sling and hit the Philistine in the forehead. The stone sank in, and Goliath stumbled and fell face down on the ground.

It was the 1985 championship game, Villanova 66, Georgetown 64. The Wildcats played a near perfect game, shooting 78% to stun the Big East rival and top-ranked Hoyas, who were double-digit favorites. This Championship game in 1983, which resulted in North Carolina State beating Houston 54-52, future NBA Superstars and Hall-of-Famers Hakeem Olajuwon and Clyde "The Glide" Drexler were supposed to dominate. However, Jim Valvano's NCSU Wolfpack had other dreams. First his team had to fight just to get invited to the "big dance" by winning the ACC tournament. Then in one of the NCAA's most memorable moments ever, forward Lorenzo Charles followed up Derek Whitenberg's air ball at the buzzer for the victory. What did those winning teams have in common? First, they each won a championship, and secondly, before each contest started they were considered to be the underdog.

It's an attitude that says, "I can't," instead of, "I can." Is the "I can't" attitude in your locker room? Half your team's battle in preparing to be successful is in their minds; your players must know they can win against any team regardless of their circumstances, their opponent's ability, or their reputation. Philippians 4:13 reminds us that we can do *all* things through Christ who strengthens us. If God said it, that's good enough for me! Now it's up to me as a believer-coach to instill that mindset into my players and support staff.

It was the young David who had to remind his older counterparts of this truth when he said, "greater is He that is within you than he that is within the world." David's relatively size didn't matter; his age didn't matter; only the size of his heart and his belief in his God mattered. Some may have said that he bordered on cockiness, but I like to think of it as having unrelenting confidence. He was confronted with the task of being the "front man" for an entire country. Imagine Shaquille O'Neil and add an additional two feet in height. That was Goliath, the champion from Gath, the hero of the Philistines. David didn't run or hide from the challenge. In fact, he faced it "head on." When everyone was backing down, he was stepping up! Victories cannot be achieved by the "faint of heart," and after your victories have been won, if the world wants to call them upsets ... well, that's their prerogative, but we know the difference.

THE COACHES' CORNER

QUESTION AND ANSWER SESSION FEATURING:

Joe Gugliero, Women's Basketball Coach

Gerald Davis: Do you remember your most memorable win?
Joe Gugliero: In May of 1996 I coached a thirteen-year-old AAU team that qualified for the AAU Nationals. The team was comprised of some very special kids and parents who, to this day, make up a large part of my fondest coaching memories. The kids were totally eager to learn and I was passionate about teaching ... it was a match made in heaven. Their parents were some of the finest people I'd ever met – level headed, hands-off, and highly cooperative. I am still good friends with several of them. The team had been together for three years when I was assigned to coach them. They were talented but undisciplined. The coach that had worked with them for the previous three years had done an outstanding job of feeding their competitive instincts and making them very passionate about the game. All I had to do was teach them fundamentals and team concepts. The team had come very close to winning the District AAU championships the previous two years but fell short both years in the semi-finals. So the kids had a burning desire to go to the Nationals the year I took over the helm. Oh yeah, I forgot to mention that the Nationals were being held at Disney that year ... I'm sure that had a lot to do with their high level of desire! The kids worked very hard and improved dramatically in games and practice sessions leading up to the district championships. We went undefeated in several high level tournaments leading up to the Districts and beat a couple of nationally ranked teams in the process.

Here's another interesting side note; at the time I ascribed our success to "great coaching." I have been humbled since that time and now realize that it was all about what the kids brought to the table. Anyway, we were riding high going into the Districts. We won our first two games easily, pulled out a buzzer beater in our third match-up, and got knocked down into the loser's bracket in our 4th game against a team we had beaten easily in an earlier tournament. The next game we played was the loser's bracket final, with the winner advancing to the championship round versus the winner of the winner's bracket and a guarantee of an invite to the Nationals (two teams were guaranteed spots that year). Our opponent in that game was the Liberty Belles, a highly skilled, determined and well coached team from Queens. The game was a seesaw affair from the get go. With 3 minutes to go the Belles opened a 7-point lead that seemed insurmountable.

I decided to extend our defense and let it fly. Don't ask me how it happened, but our kids bumped up their level of intensity and, within a minute and a half, we had tied the game. We went on to win the game by 6, going on a 13-0 run during the last 3 minutes of the game. The game was thrilling but it was the reaction of the kids and parents after the game that touched me most. They were crying, hugging, laughing ... it was a great moment that has not been matched since.

Gerald Davis: What was your pre-game speech like?

Joe Gugliero: I was much more demonstrative back then ... I'm older and a bit more methodical now. I remember sitting the kids down in a little nook hidden at the end of a hallway just outside of Christ the King's gymnasium (where the game was played). I could see how nervous they were. Unfortunately, I was just as nervous as they were, but I did my best to hide it and to assure them that they had it in them to win the game. After explaining what I believed we needed to do to win the game from a technical standpoint, I attempted to appeal to their hearts and souls. I talked about the power of togetherness and reminded them of the definition of success we had adopted as a team (which I still ascribe to). I told them that if they stuck together, executed what they had learned and gave everything they had to the game, they would be winners no matter what the score ended up being. When you approach winning in this manner it takes all of the pressure off of you. Success is completely within the realm of your control. When you take that mindset, success becomes a choice, not an uncertain event. Now, do I believe that my words had any impact on the kids? I don't know. In all probability the prospect of being at Disney held much more weight in their minds than my words.

Gerald Davis: What was the post-game celebration like?

Joe Gugliero: Mayhem and pandemonium, kids and parents hugging and kissing, and so on. I took a step back from it all and really enjoyed it as both a spectator and participant. I kept the post-game meeting brief but it was highly emotional. I told the kids how proud I was about the nature of the comeback and about the spirit and character it revealed in them. I told them I loved them, and then said some special words about the kids who did not get much playing time that day. I left the gym, went home to my wife, and reveled in the glory of victory and the prospect of future conquests. Little did I know that I had reached the top of the mountain earlier that day and that everything that followed in my coaching career would be an attempt to re-capture the special moments of that splendid spring day.

3-POINTERS

Genesis 21:5 (NASB) – Now Abraham was one hundred years old when his son Isaac was born to him.

1 John 5:4 (KJV) – For whatsoever is born of God overcometh the world: and this is the victory that overcometh the world, even our faith.

1 Corinthians 15:57 (KJV) – But thanks be to God, which giveth us the victory through our Lord Jesus Christ.

BUZZER BEATER

Our destiny changes with our thoughts; we shall become what we wish to become, do what we wish to do, when our habitual thoughts correspond with our desires.

- Orison Swett Marden

POST-GAME NOTES

....

....

....

....

....

....

....

2nd QUARTER:

Rebounding ... from mistakes

In our profession, when you talk about rebounding, you think in terms of retrieving an offensive or defensive shot. The term rebounding in this books speaks of a reaction to a setback or frustration or, as singer Donnie McClurkin says it best in his song "We Fall Down" when he admonishes the believer not to stay down when transgressions have been committed but instead to just get back up and understand that we serve a loving and forgiving God. Those of us who are coaches are like any other individual – we're not perfect even though we strive to be. Here in the 2nd Quarter of this book we will see how our wrong choices or mistakes don't have to be our undoing.

If it weren't for God's grace, where would mankind be? Who else would've been willing to sacrifice their life for us other than Jesus? Remember, we are talking about an innocent man who went to the cross for every sin imaginable, "Who was delivered for our offences, and raised again for our justification" (Romans 4:25).

No sin is too big or too small that we cannot go to the Father and ask for His forgiveness. Now *that's* the kind of God I serve! That's why God the Father doesn't want His people to wallow in self-pity when we make mistakes (and we will make mistakes). When you're in that self-pity mode, the deceiver will try to bring you down even lower spiritually. He'll stay on your mind and try to place all kinds of negative thoughts in there – particularly thoughts that you're not worthy of God's love or forgiveness – but, you are. God loves us that much! In Luke 23:39-43 we read of the thief who was being crucified on the cross next to Jesus, and his faith allowed him to walk in that forgiveness, which therefore allowed him to be in paradise the moment he died.

However, the other criminal mocked Christ and he didn't pursue the forgiveness that Christ has made available for all who repent with a sincere heart.

When things are going wrong on the basketball court, it's easy to "pack it up" and call it quits; it's difficult to try harder to do the things necessary to get back into the game with the hope of eventually pulling out a victory, but that's what every team needs to do in order to succeed. The easy way out could be conducting yourself like the disrespectful thief – by doing and saying things that don't exhibit REBOUNDING, but God wants us to humble ourselves, admit when we're wrong, and then get right back in the game!

CHOICES ... *the act of choosing; selections we've made*

Read: John 11:45-57

Key Verses: John 11:49-50 – *And one of them, Caiaphas, who was High Priest that year, said, "You stupid idiots let this one man die for the people – why should the whole nation perish?"*

In every profession choices are made daily that affect individuals. The responsibilities of decision makers should not be taken lightly because in some cases, life or death can lie in the balance. In the arena of sports, "in-game" decisions may not rank on such a high scale. For a coach, some life-changing decisions being made by our players can be classified as such. While final decisions are ultimately in the hands of the individual, a coach can play a large role in those important life choices.

Caiaphas, a High Priest for the Sadducees and a very pompous, wealthy politician, made a number of irresponsible choices. He hated Jesus and wanted Him dead at all costs. He was fearful that Jesus' kingdom message would affect his wealth and hurt his position in society. Therefore, he was a major player in Jesus' capture and crucifixion.

As coaches, we all want to win, but we should not want it so badly that we're willing to sacrifice the integrity of our eternal soul. The choices we make for the team, player, high school, or university should be the kind that we can reflect about in the future without guilt or shame.

THE COACHES' CORNER

QUESTION AND ANSWER SESSION FEATURING:

Bobbi Jo Austin, Women's Basketball Coach

Gerald Davis: If you had to make the choice between an excellent point guard or an excellent post player, which would you rather choose?

Bobbi Jo Austin: That is an interesting question. I think I would probably choose an excellent big girl. I think both positions are most important, but a big girl allows for an inside presence on both sides of the ball. It also allows for rebounding, which I believe is a major key in winning games. I like that a post player with presence will have to garner attention in the post. Thus guards can get off some uncontested shots. If you look at the teams in the 2006 NCAA tournament, it was those teams that had the stronger inside presence that did damage. The championship game with the University of North Carolina versus the University of Maryland was a perfect example. While both teams had tremendous big girls it was UMD who were just a little more aggressive ... even though UNC probably had the best point guard in the country on their team.

Gerald Davis: If you had to make the choice between an excellent scorer or an excellent defender, which would you choose?

Bobbi Jo Austin: This question is a little more difficult. However, I'm going to choose – the defender. I believe that a good defender's attitude can be contagious. The electricity can travel throughout the team, which can bring about positive results. Defense can be a very powerful weapon and can throw even the best teams off their games.

3-POINTERS

Proverbs 4:7 (KJV) – *Wisdom is the principal thing; therefore get wisdom: and with all thy getting get understanding.*

Proverbs 15:21 (KJV) – *Folly is joy to him that is destitute of wisdom: but a man of understanding walketh uprightly.*

Proverbs 28:26 (KJV) – *He that trusteth in his own heart is a fool: but whoso walketh wisely, he shall be delivered.*

BUZZER BEATER

In forty hours I shall be in battle; with little information and on the spur of the moment I will have to make the most momentous decisions. But I believe that one's spirit enlarges with responsibility, and that, with God's help, I shall make them, and make them right.

- General George S. Patton

POST-GAME NOTES

....
....
....
....
....
....
....

COMPASSION ... *the feeling one has for another's sorrow or hardship*

Read: Luke 5:17-25

Key Verses: Luke 5:18-19 – *Then – look! Some men came carrying a paralyzed man on a sleeping mat. They tried to push through the crowd to Jesus but couldn't reach him. So they went up on the roof above him, took off some tiles, and lowered the sick man down into the crowd, still on his sleeping mat, right in front of Jesus.*

Is there any place for compassion or empathy in the game of basketball, or is it necessary to pummel your opponent regardless of the situation, time, or score? For some coaches, a lopsided score doesn't matter. Whether there are 10 minutes on the game clock or 2 minutes, if pressing is a part of their defensive identity, they will continue until the final buzzer. For some it's an inherent part of their mindset or personality to not allow their coaching philosophy to be altered regardless of the score, but does that make it right? In my humble opinion, there will be situations during the course of a game when you can "loosen the reins" just a little bit. It doesn't make you non-aggressive or a terrible coach if you decide not to press when you're winning by 20-plus points with under 5 minutes to play. It simply makes you someone with a little compassion and sportsmanship.

One of the New Testament Gospels was written by a man named Luke, who was a trained physician by trade and an appointed disciple by Jesus Christ. (He also wrote the book of Acts.) Luke was also a man of compassion. I'm sure if Luke were a ball player today he would extend a hand to help a fallen opponent. Why? Partly because of what a doctor is by definition. Furthermore, as a disciple of Christ, his responsibility of sharing and living the way of the Gospel falls right within the framework of being compassionate. Being a man of compassion, he was compelled to share. Finally, he was also Paul's traveling companion as the apostle made his third missionary journey. It's only an uncompassionate and selfish individual who would keep the good news of the Gospel to themselves.

THE COACHES' CORNER

QUESTION AND ANSWER SESSION FEATURING:

Pat Torney, Head Varsity Boy's Basketball Coach, and Head Varsity Baseball Coach

Gerald Davis: How do you handle cutting players at try-outs?

Pat Torney: I always tell the whole group that the cutting process is the one I like least about coaching. I tell them that the best players don't always make the team, and that how they conduct themselves off the court also has an effect on whether they will make the team. I will usually take a few days to investigate borderline possibilities in school and them post a list on the bulletin board of the players who make the team.

Gerald Davis: You're pounding a team 58-20 with 5 minutes left. How would you lessen the embarrassment for your opponents, or would you?

Pat Torney: That's an easy one. Clear the bench; sit back in a zone; no fast breaks. Having been on both sides of that situation, I wish more people would abide by that.

3-POINTERS

John 8:7 (KJV) – So when they continued asking him, he lifted up himself, and said unto them, He that is without sin among you, let him first cast a stone at her.

Lamentations 3:22 (NASB) – The Lord's lovingkindness indeed never ceases, for his compassions never fail.

Ephesians 4:31 (KJV) – Let all bitterness, and wrath, and clamor, and evil speaking, be put away from you.

BUZZER BEATER

We cannot live only for ourselves. A thousand fibers connect us with our fellow men.

- Herman Melville

POST-GAME NOTES

....
....
....
....
....
....
....

FAVORITES ... *liked better than others; liked very much*

Read: Acts 10: 1-48

Key Verses: Acts 10:34-35 – *Then Peter replied, "I see very clearly that the Jews are not God's only favorites! In every nation he has those who worship him do good deeds and are acceptable to him.*

My wife and I are the proud parents of three children: Christina, my eldest, and Bryan and Brandon, who are twins – and we love them all the same. Ask any parent that same question and I'm sure the percentages would lean heavily toward them also loving their children equally. Where degrees of love can vary with human beings, even among parents in the love they have for their children, the percentage with Jesus Christ is always the same 100%. He unequivocally loves all His children the same. He has no favorites!

Coach ... do you have favorites on your team? Is there a player whom you permit to do certain things that the others are not allowed to do? If God doesn't have favorites, you shouldn't either. I'm sure there's a coach reading this right now and asking, "Yeah, but what about my superstar?" Well, let me ask you this: Is the superstar bigger than the team? There are instances where you may ask or require certain players to perform certain tasks based on their gifts, talents, and abilities, but that's different because you're asking this of them in an effort to do what's best for the team.

God has no favorites, and He proved this aspect of Himself in the case of Peter, a Jew, and Cornelius, a Gentle. Nearly 2,000 years ago many Jews believed that the gospel was only for them. Their laws and customs didn't even allow them to interact with or fellowship with Gentiles. Peter had reservations about sharing the gospel with Gentiles until he received a vision from God that he was to travel to Caesarea, the capital of a Roman province in Judea, to meet with Cornelius. Cornelius was a Roman officer in the Centurion army and was a good man, but he wasn't saved, although he was seeking the truth. It was God who wanted the gospel made available to Cornelius and to everyone who desires a relationship with Him, Jew and Gentile alike.

THE COACHES' CORNER

QUESTION AND ANSWER SESSION FEATURING:

Brenda Morgan, Head Varsity Basketball Coach, Abraham Lincoln H. S., Brooklyn, NY

Gerald Davis: Have you ever been accused of having a favorite?

Brenda Morgan: I try to be fair, and I also try to see the uniqueness in all of my players. I'm always reminded of Psalm 115:12 where the psalmist says, "The Lord has been mindful of us; He will bless us." So it's not only about coaching – it's about tapping into that uniqueness of what God has created. Developing strengths in my players is a challenge for me because I am somewhat of a perfectionist. However, I must admit I have had favorites. It's natural to favor the "go to" person because they're dependable, and you can always count on them to deliver and get the job done. I've been blessed to have "go to" players with beautiful humble personalities.

Another scripture I love is Proverbs 13:13-15 (NIV): "He who scorns instruction will pay for it, but he who respects a command is rewarded. The teaching of the wise is a fountain of life, turning a man from the snares of death. Good understanding wins favor, but the way of the unfaithful is hard."

Gerald Davis: What qualities about those favorite go-to players stood out to you the most?

Brenda Morgan: Humility is key. Other qualities that made these players stand out were their ability to listen and follow instructions, and their interpersonal communication skills; these qualities create a special kind of bond between coach and player. Believing that "specificity is the grounds for cooperation," it is of the utmost importance that each player knows clearly what his or her roles are. We have open dialogue as a team, and they are well informed of their roles, what is expected of them, what's acceptable, and what's unacceptable. "Expectation sets the atmosphere for miracles; expectation also causes preparation, and preparation produces confidence." It's amazing how these players rise to meet the challenge of what is set before them. I try to the best of my ability to instill in them the belief that everyone is an important and integral part of the team, from the starting five, to the tenth person off the bench, to the person who fills the water bottles; from the jump ball to encouraging each other while on the bench during winning and losing. It's truly a process. When the groundwork is laid about what I stand for, it's a little easier. However, there are always issues when dealing with teenagers and their changing personalities and feelings.

Gerald Davis: How difficult is it to discipline the players who are usually the good, dependable ones?

Brenda Morgan: Disciplining is always difficult no matter who is on the receiving end, but I've found that when they know what I stand for, they are much harder on themselves than I could ever be. It's more uncomfortable for the player because I'm not there to judge; it's more like they know they've disappointed me as well as their team. I'm really tough, but most of them understand that kind of tough love, because oftentimes "coach" represents more than just the team coaching that takes place during practices and games. Also, because of the closeness I have with my athletes, they know I want what's best for them. I often meditate on Philippians 4:13, "I can do all things through Christ who strengthens me," and I truly believe in the axiom, "God's work done God's way will never lack His supply." And so, when I have to do things that are not so popular, I pray that they will see Christ in me.

3-POINTERS

James 2:5 (NASB) – Listen, my beloved brethren: did not God choose the poor of this world to be rich in faith and heirs of the kingdom which he promised to those who love him?

James 2:8-9 (NASB) – If, however, you are fulfilling the royal law, according to the scripture, "You shall love your neighbor as yourself," you are doing well But if you show partiality, you are committing sin and are convicted by the law as transgressors.

Genesis 37:3-4 (KJV) – Now Israel loved Joseph more than all his children, because he was the son of his old age: and he made him a coat of many colours. And when his brethren saw that their father loved him more than all his brethren, they hated him, and could not speak peaceably unto him.

BUZZER BEATER

Only recruit players you want to coach.

\- Tony Demeo

POST-GAME NOTES

. . . .

. . . .

. . . .

. . . .

. . . .

··

··

MISTAKES ... *a wrong action or statement proceeding from faulty judgment, inadequate knowledge, or inattention*

Read: Acts 15: 36-41

Key Verse: Proverbs 28:13 – *A man who refuses to admit his mistakes can never be successful. But if he confesses and forsakes them, he gets another chance.*

The good thing about sports is that after the final whistle of a game, there is usually another game to look forward to and prepare for (unless of course it's the final game of the season). This means that there is always a chance to redeem yourself after a mistake is made. Most importantly, setting your sights on winning another upcoming game gives you and your team an opportunity to learn from the mistakes you've made. There was only one perfect individual who walked this earth, and His name was Jesus Christ. Everyone else is prone to mistakes. It doesn't matter how many times you go over the scouting reports or tapes, you just might miss something such as not calling a timeout or calling a play when you should have. Read my lips – you are not perfect and you *will* make another mistake – I guarantee it! So, don't beat yourself over the head about it. Learn from those mistakes and move on ... unless of course you desire to be the poster child for Rolaids.

Mistakes weren't foreign to Mark, Jesus' disciple who would later become one of the apostles. He had trouble staying committed to a task. However, Paul, his missionary partner on one mission trip, wouldn't let him forget it. The first team consisted of Paul, Barnabas, and Mark. For whatever reason, Mark abruptly abandons the team, which Paul remembered when it came time for the second missionary trip. He refused Mark's re-admission to the team. The Bible doesn't document reasons for Mark's departure but he may have been homesick. Thus, the matter of his maturity and professionalism also came into question.

Making mistakes is a part of the game of life and basketball. It's what you do to rectify the situation *after* the mistake is made that sets you apart and determines whether you'll be a success or a failure. "Dust yourself off and try again" – It's more than a cliché old saying; it should be your way of life and mode of operation.

As it turned out, Mark must have rectified those past indiscretions because he did travel on another missionary trip with Barnabas two years later.

THE COACHES' CORNER

"One Mistake too Many"

Clarice Bell, Former Player – Women's Basketball, The City College of New York, NY, NY

Nobody enjoys losing, but the worst loss is one that you were supposed to win. Emotions are running high; you're disappointed, embarrassed, angry, and frustrated, especially when many of the mistakes could have been prevented. During the course of the game your heart races, adrenaline is pumping and you're constantly looking at the clock thinking about how many points you need to catch up. You are yelling at your teammate to pass the ball because you're wide open; but instead, they decide to drive in the middle of three defenders. The point guard is making careless passes because she is tired from hanging out too late the night before.

Now it's half time. You run off court to the locker room thinking *I'm a senior, this is it, this may be the last game I ever play for the school again.* The coach explains the half-time adjustments and each player goes around and speaks about their efforts for the first half and what they plan to do for the second half. You talk about the mistakes made and how to fix them; you begin your chant –

"Whose house? C's house!"

"Whose house? C's house!"

"Whose house" C's house!"

"ONE, TWO, THREE, CITY!"

Now you are all pumped and ready to go win this game so you can go on to win the CUNY championship, but the second half is worse than the first. There are more missed lay-ups, more careless passes, more nonchalant dribbles down the court – that all equals up to more points for the other team.

You practice all year long for the playoffs, which you *know* you can win. Individually you are better. On paper you are better as a team; you are better, but you're not proving it on the basketball court.

You continue to play hard because you know this could be the end. At least you can go on and say, "I gave 100 percent." But somehow that still isn't good enough. Your heart burns; you feel the tears accumulating, waiting to run down your face. It hurts so badly because you should have won ... and you know that the team you spent more time with than your own family made too many mistakes to win.

QUESTION AND ANSWER SESSION FEATURING:

Ronald Moore, Former NBA Player, Men's Basketball Semi-pro Coach and Head Women's Basketball Coach.

Gerald Davis: Suppose a player has just made a mistake that has caused a defeat. How do you address the situation with that player and your team?

Ronald Moore: If a player makes a mistake that costs the game, my approach is to make that player feel as if he or she is still part of the success of the team and that one play does not win or lose games. I approach my team in the same way to get them to understand that the mistakes that were made earlier in the game are the ones that hurt our chances of winning that particular game, and then I remind them how important it is to maintain a positive mental focus for an entire game.

Gerald Davis: Mistakes are a part of the game, but which aspect of the game – offense or defense – are you less tolerant of?

Ronald Moore: As a coach I believe that the difference between winning and losing is determined by defense. In basketball anyone can have an "off game" offensively. You can execute the offense to perfection, but there will be games when the ball just won't go in the basket. However, there is one thing that I cannot tolerate – and that is bad defense. I have witnessed and been a part of games where a team's defensive pressure has created points in clusters. When a team is struggling offensively, it can jump-start a team to victory.

3-POINTERS

Genesis 4:7 (NASB) – *If you do well, will not your countenance be lifted up? And if you do not do well, sin is crouching at the door; and its desire is for you, but you must master it."*

Proverbs 28:13 (NASB) – *He who conceals his transgressions will not prosper, but he who confesses and forsakes them will find compassion.*

1 John 5:4 (NKJV) – *For whatever is born of God overcomes the world. And this is the victory that has overcome the world – our faith.*

BUZZER BEATER

Only he who does nothing makes no mistakes.

- French Proverb

POST-GAME NOTES

....
....
....
....
....
....
....

PATIENCE ... *willingness to put up with waiting, pain, and trouble while remaining calm; endurance without complaining or losing self-control*

Read: 2 Thessalonians 1:1-12

Key Verse: 2 Thessalonians 1:5 – *This is only one example of the fair, just way God does things, for he is using your sufferings to make you ready for his Kingdom.*

Of all the attributes a good coach needs to have, patience is an absolute must, from Biddie Ball to the professional ranks. A coach cannot consider himself a coach without being able to conduct himself with restraint on many different levels and in many different situations. From in-game situations to dealing with personality conflicts to the daily day-to-day operations of a basketball program, problems will arise that will require a level head, understanding, and above all – patience.

Patience is a trait that has to be worked on or prayed about. Some are blessed with the good fortune of having it ingrained in their nature, and some have to work on being more patient. Peter was an individual who fell into the latter category. Peter was a fisherman by trade and a good man. However, like every human being, he had some flaws. At times he could be accused of being a little brash and a tad-bit impulsive. His personality was also that of a "go-getter" – the type who, when faced with a task, believes there is only one way to accomplish that task – and that's at full speed! Sometimes when you're going at full speed, however, you might miss a few things.

Consider the possible consequences that might result if you don't exercise patience in your coaching:

- Always think first before you act, and understand that your words or actions can lead to final results that you may not want.

Conduct mental and physical patience exercises

- Take a deep breath. As you exhale, extinguish each and every negative thought you have about a particular situation you're dealing with. Take a moment to think about how you can handle that situation differently, especially if it will affect the outcome positively.

Think empathy ... to evoke patience

- Place yourself in the position of the one who is on the receiving end of your message. Is what you're saying constructive? Did you say it tactfully?

THE COACHES' CORNER

QUESTION AND ANSWER SESSION FEATURING:

Deborah Mortley, Head Varsity Girl's Basketball Coach, Bishop Loughlin Memorial H. S, Brooklyn, NY

Gerald Davis: Have you experienced any losing seasons while coaching?

Deborah Mortley: Yes, I have experienced losing seasons, and I have also learned to set goals that are attainable. When winning is not feasible, small objectives must be understood by all involved; accomplishments are then measured by what we as a team can achieve.

Gerald Davis: How did you grow as a coach from those experiences?

Deborah Mortley: As a coach I've learned to accept my players and their talent for what it is. I am here to help them grow as individuals and to become productive in a society that will take them into the 21st century. The attitude of winning at all costs has placed a heavy burden on our society. That type of mindset must be changed if we want to produce quality people.

3-POINTERS

2 Thessalonians 1:4 (KJV) – *So that we ourselves glory in you in the churches of God for your patience and faith in all your persecutions and tribulations that ye endure.*

Nehemiah 9:17 (NASB) – *And they refused to listen, and did not remember thy wondrous deeds which thou hadst perfomed among them; so they became stubborn and appointed a leader to return to their slavery in Egypt. But thou art a God of forgiveness, gracious and compassionate, slow to anger, and abounding in lovingkindness; and thou didst not forsake them.*

Isaiah 40:31 (NKJV) – *But those who wait on the Lord shall renew their strength; they shall mount up with wings like eagles, they shall run and not be weary, they shall walk and not faint.*

BUZZER BEATER

Great things are not done by impulse, but by a series of small things brought together.

-Vincent Van Gogh

POST-GAME NOTES

....
....
....
....
....
....
....

REBUILDING ... *the process of building again*

Read: Nehemiah 2:11-20

Key Verse: Nehemiah 2:17 – *But now I told them, "You know full well the tragedy of our city; it lies in ruins and its gates are burned. Let us rebuild the wall of Jerusalem and rid ourselves of this disgrace!"*

Nehemiah humbly began as a cupbearer for the Persian King Artaxexes. The cupbearer's job was a difficult and dangerous one. Some may have considered it to be a glamorous job based on the closeness that was needed between a king and his cupbearer. However, there was a hazardous side to this position. As a matter of fact, life and death could lie in the balance. The cupbearer was the food and drink taster before anything touched the lips of the king; in case someone was trying to poison the king, the cupbearer would die instead. Therefore, the trust/respect factor had to be in full effect – and understandably so!

In reading the biblical story of his life, it becomes evident that Nehemiah was an honorable man. He was spiritually led by God to leave his good job in Persia, which provided him with excellent benefits. He felt compelled to go to Jerusalem to rebuild the walls and gates of that holy city.

The rebuilding of the walls was of great importance for the safety and security of Jerusalem. Nehemiah's innate abilities as an organizer, motivator, and problem solver got the job done in a mere 52 days. It was a tremendous undertaking and thus an amazing accomplishment, but God was with Nehemiah.

It also takes a certain attitude to build something from nothing. I have always admired architects, engineers, builders, and masons. My Dad was a skillful bricklayer in New York who built many well-known city landscapes. I was also able to see his handiwork first-hand on our two-story home in Brooklyn.

Witnessing the finished product done by people like Nehemiah and my dad is very pleasing to the eye. Now, if you were to interview those visionaries, I'm sure they would tell you that the thrill lies in first having a strategy, idea, or concept and then seeing it come alive right before their eyes; however, not until after they've experienced some sleepless nights, a little anxiety, or financial challenges. Nevertheless, they overcame these difficulties and now they have a story to tell. If they had pursued those projects without the correct mental and physical attitude, most of their ideas would remain just that – merely ideas. Many inspirational stories have been written about men and women from the sports world, the business arena, or even from the next-door neighbor and their world-changing ways. They all had one thing in common: they never backed down from a challenge.

The classified job ads for basketball coaching positions in April and May are filled from top to bottom. These positions are made available through retirement, firings, or the need for a coach who has the qualifications to rebuild and turn a program around. It takes a special individual to restore a losing situation to prominence. It also takes patience and endurance, but most of all **talented** players who understand the concept of **teamwork** and a coach who's inner drive screams **tenacity**! Are you that builder?

Players and Coaches' Building Blocks for Success:

Teachable
Thoughtful
Tactful
Aggressive
Effort
Efficient
Leadership
Attitude
No-nonsense
Enthusiasm
Moral
Attentive
Noble
Winner
Communicator

Trustworthy
Obedient
Intelligent

Responsible
Thinker

Knowledge
Youthful

THE COACHES' CORNER

QUESTION AND ANSWER SESSION FEATURING:

Deborah Mortley, Head Varsity Girl's Basketball Coach, Bishop Loughlin Memorial H. S, Brooklyn, NY

Gerald Davis: Which would you prefer coaching, a team with less talent that has to be nurtured or a ready-made contender?
Deborah Mortley: I have had the pleasure of working with both the talented and the not so talented, and I know it is far easier to work with talented players. I think any coach who says he/she would prefer to work with less talented players definitely has the gift of patience.

3-POINTERS

Romans 7:4 (NASB) – Therefore, my brethren, you also were made to die to the law through the body to another, to him who was raised from the dead, that we might bear fruit for God.

Luke 5.37 (NASB) – And no one puts new wine into old wine skins; otherwise the new wine will burst the skins, and it will be spilled out, and the skins will be ruined.

Isaiah 43:18-19 (KJV) – Remember ye not the former things, neither consider the things of old. Behold, I will do a new thing..."

BUZZER BEATER

If you are afraid for your future, you don't have a present.

- James Petersen

POST-GAME NOTES

....
....
....
....
....
....
....

SECOND CHANCES ... *are opportunities*

Read: 2 Chronicles 33:1-19

Key Verse: 2 Chronicles 33:12 – *Then at last he came to his senses and cried out humbly to God for help.*

King Manasseh's reign was filled with nothing less than chaos, turmoil, and desecration for the things of God. He succeeded his father, King Hezekiah, who was a faithful king and more in tune with being obedient. You would think that Manasseh would follow the same path of righteousness. However, evil and rebellion resonated throughout the kingdom. It was Manasseh who filled the courts of the temple with idols. The people were even encouraged to worship pagan gods, which they consulted on a consistent basis. Finally he did something that most would consider to be unforgivable: he sacrificed his own children. Nonetheless, God's forgiveness is far-reaching regardless of the sin. When it comes to second chances, mankind can be limited. God takes great pleasure in forgiving a sincere and repentant heart because God is a God of second chances. It took a little bit of time for Manasseh to come to his senses, but he did eventually cry out for God's help. I have often thought about what would be my breaking point when it comes to forgiving. Thankfully for myself and for King Manasseh, God has already given his children the "How-To Guide for Forgiveness and Second Chances."

As a coach, situations can occur during the season that put you in a position where you have to either dole out severe punishment or administer a second chance. It's one of the toughest assignments a coach has. It's also a process that must be done with complete objectivity. Some of the questions that must be asked are: Was the situation a blatant disregard for rules and regulations? After all the checks and balances have been considered, what will the end result be? A decision has to be made as to whether a second chance will be given. Above all – the coach is responsible to give second chances for all the right reasons. It's paramount that common sense, morality, and righteousness prevail in every decision. What *shouldn't* be mixed into the equation is how the possible suspension or expulsion of a player(s) will affect a game, a season, or winning in general.

THE COACHES' CORNER

QUESTION AND ANSWER SESSION FEATURING:

Pat Torney, Head Varsity Boy's Basketball, Head Varsity Boy's Baseball Coach

Gerald Davis: How quick is your "hook" for substitutions when a player makes a mistake?

Pat Torney: It depends on the mistake. If a player misses a dunk or slaps the board on a lay-up and misses, he comes out on the very next whistle. If the mistake is the result of a hustle play, I usually don't take him out at all. Giving up baseline on defense a second time will usually result in a hook. It depends on whether or not I have someone who can replace him adequately, although the dunk/slap board rule is always enforced.

3-POINTERS

Luke 15:20 (NASB) – *And he got up and came to his father. But while he was still a long way off, his father saw him, and felt compassion for him, and ran and embraced him, and kissed him.*

Isaiah 43:18-19 (KJV) – *Remember ye not the former things, neither consider the things of old. Behold, I will do a new thing.*

Psalm 51:10 (NIV) – *Create in me a pure heart, O God, and renew a steadfast spirit within me.*

BUZZER BEATER

To err is human, to forgive divine.

- Alexander Pope

POST-GAME NOTES

....
....
....
....
....
....
....

HALFTIME

Billy Donovan – University of Florida

Bruce Webber – University of Illinois

Jay Wright – University of Villanova

Jeff Ruland – Former Head Men's Basketball Coach Iona College my sons (L) Bryan and (R) Brandon

Jeff Van Gundy – Former New York Knicks Head Coach

Jim Boeheim – Syracuse University

Johnny Dawkins – Standford University

Brandon and Bryan Davis – Summer League Basketball Team: Agape House

Tom Izzo – Michigan State University

Tommy Amaker – Harvard University

Jim Colhoun – University of Connecticut

3rd QUARTER:

Ball Handling ... Cousey, Kidd, Magic, and Nash all rolled into one

The "floor general" ... the "captain of the ship" ... "the coach on the floor" ... are some accurate ways to describe a point guard. Their responsibilities at times are usually greater than the others. Not only must they have complete knowledge of what they're doing on the court, but also, it's wise for them to know where each player is supposed to be on the floor as well. Moreover, the mental demands on the point guard can be taxing, but that comes with the territory of the position.

It has often been said that, "as a point guard goes – so goes the team." Can you imagine the LA Lakers of the 1980s being the same dynamic team without Earvin "Magic" Johnson? Yet while Magic was an exceptional talent, the quality that made him different from other guards in his era was his ability to process a play in seconds before its actual development. Thus, his cerebral gifts at times exceeded his basketball skills.

As Christian believers, it is not at all unusual that we must juggle with the daily challenges that life will bring us and, like a point guard who is taught to lead in a manner that exudes confidence while running a team, we too can do more than one thing at once and be good at it, whether it's in the work place, at home, or on the basketball court. We can handle it because the spirit of the Lord is with us. In basketball circles we call it "handles" (dribbling expertise). In the believer's glossary it is referred to as the Fruit of the Spirit: *But when the Holy Spirit controls our lives he will produce this kind of fruit in us: love, joy, peace, patience, kindness, goodness, faithfulness, gentleness, and self-control* (Galatians 5:22-23).

The good thing about being on God's team is that our Savior first exemplified the characteristics that are listed above. If we would only initiate and practice those traits, the pressure situations of life wouldn't be merely tolerable – they would be a slam-dunk!

As you read this chapter, know that Jesus Christ has empowered you to succeed in all things and at all times!

ENDURE/ENDURANCE ... *the power to last or to keep on*

Read: Jeremiah 1:1-19

Key Verse: Jeremiah 1:8 – *And don't be afraid of the people, for I, the Lord, will be with you and see you through.*

Not many high schools or colleges have the luxury of hiring a strength and conditioning coach. The benefits of their skills and instruction outweigh any disadvantages in cost, however. Even when conventional thinking might suggest that such a position is unnecessary, sports is a big business, and it's very important to keep players in their best physical condition. There was a time when limited stretching and exercising was all that was needed prior to participating in team sports. Not anymore! Like everything else, strength and conditioning in sports is a science, and it's advancing to an entirely different level. The athlete who's in the best physical condition is more likely to outperform the player who's not. As a coach, that's my hope – to be the better conditioned team, especially during "end game" situations. It's a bad visual when you see players bent over gasping for breath. It's usually the physically fit, endurance-trained team that endures competition both physically and mentally, and thus enjoys the fruits of victory.

Endurance was one of Jeremiah's more enduring traits. That's why the prophet Jeremiah had to be in shape both physically, spiritually, and mentally: to withstand the many trials and tribulations for

God. For 40 years Jeremiah courageously proclaimed the Word of God! During that time period, no one was listening! Not the kings, priests, or even Jeremiah's own family. He was rejected, persecuted, and even imprisoned. Yet Jeremiah's compassion and concern for God's people went unmatched. He has even been referred to as the "weeping prophet." His emotions notwithstanding, Jeremiah kept on purging evil and doing what was asked of him. He understood that the mark of endurance is allowing your faith in God to supersede the negative situations that seem unbearable and insurmountable. Like Jeremiah, we need to remember that with God, all things are possible.

THE COACHES' CORNER

QUESTION AND ANSWER SESSION FEATURING:

Mark Coluccio, Fitness Trainer

Gerald Davis: What are some common mistakes an athlete makes when they're trying to get in condition?
Mark Coluccio:

1. Not maintaining a proper diet
2. Not getting enough rest
3. Not following a **sound** and **structured** regimen for strength training and cardiovascular training.
4. Not warming up and cooling down properly during workout sessions.

Athletes must consume good or "smart" carbohydrates instead of bad carbohydrates.

They should eat whole grains in order to boost energy levels. Avoid white bread, white rice, and white pasta. However, they should not eliminate carbohydrates completely because this will lead to energy deprivation. Eliminate saturated fats and trans-fats. High protein consumption is necessary for muscle and tissue strengthening. They should use low impact machines for cardiovascular activity in order to eliminate impact on the knees and back. Do cardio regularly in order to condition the heart and lungs and in order to stay lean. When strength training one cannot work the same muscle two days in a row. One must allow 48 hours to pass in order for the muscle to rebuild tissues that are torn during the strength training.

3-POINTERS

Matthew 10:22 (KJV) – *And ye shall be hated of all men for my name's sake: but he that endureth to the end shall be saved.*

2 Timothy 4:5-8 (KJV) – *But watch thou in all things, endure afflictions, do the work of an evangelist, make full proof of thy ministry. For I am now ready to be offered, and the time of my departure is at hand. I have fought a good fight, I have finished my course, I have kept the faith: Henceforth there is laid up for me a crown of righteousness, which the Lord, the righteous judge, shall give me at that day: and not to me only, but unto all them also that love his appearing.*

James 5:11 (KJV) – *Behold, we count them happy which endure; ye have heard of the patience of job, and have seen the end of the Lord; that the Lord is very pitiful, and of tender mercy.*

BUZZER BEATER

Be strong!
It matters not how deep entrenched the wrong
How hard the battle goes, the day how long
Faint not – fight on!
Tomorrow comes the song

- Maltbie D. Babcock

POST-GAME NOTES

....

....

....

....

....

....

....

FAITH ... *believing without proof; trust*

Read: Genesis 12:1-20

Key Verse: Genesis 12:1 – *God had told Abram, "Leave your own country behind you, and your own people, and go to the land I will guide you."*

At seventy-five years of age, Abram had it all. He was a wealthy landowner with a young, beautiful wife. What more could a man ask for? Life was good! Then God announced that He wanted to make a few changes – life-altering changes. Abram, being the God-fearing obedient individual that he was, undauntedly obeyed those instructions and set forth on a faith-walk journey of new beginnings.

That's the kind of unwavering faith that I want in my life – and the kind of faith that I'm trying to display at all times to my players. You shouldn't let them see you sweat; your players should not sense fear in you. Fear should not exist in your make-up or character. You could be 10 points down with two minutes remaining, your best player has fouled out, and the ref is having a bad hair day. The impossible **can** happen, but the process can only be initiated by your belief. It's a belief that comes from deep within your heart. Is it in you?

THE COACHES' CORNER

QUESTION AND ANSWER SESSION FEATURING:

Joe Gugliero, Women's Basketball Coach, AAU, H.S., New York, NY

Gerald Davis: If you could have any player from the collegiate or professional ranks of the game on the line with one shot, which one would you choose?

Joe Gugliero: Reggie Miller. The obvious answer is the track record he established during his playing days and his reputation as guy who wanted the ball when the game was on the line. What made Reggie the clutch guy he was? (a) Confidence – a confidence that was born from his God-given abilities and the countless number of hours he spent honing skills that ascended to a level few have attained; (b) Courage – a willingness to take a risk, to be the guy who might be the goat; (c) Ego/Nature of his spirit – an innate desire to be THE MAN, to be on center stage, to be the hero in an epic battle.

Gerald Davis: Tell us about one of your former players.

Joe Guegliero: Kaitlin Aggostinacchio was simply the most focused, dedicated, and intense athlete I have ever seen. Kaitlin was a very good athlete who played for me during her formidable years as a player. She was LI Catholic League Player of the Year in her senior year in high school and won a volleyball scholarship to Holy Cross University. Her offensive skills were not developed enough to play basketball at that level – at least that's what all the "experts" thought when she graduated from high school.

As it turned out, she made Holy Cross's basketball team as a walk-on and, though she saw limited playing time during her collegiate career, she eventually became captain of the team! I want her with the ball in her hands simply because of who she was. Sounds crazy, doesn't it? Most folks want the spotlight because of what the spotlight can do for them, but Kaitlin wanted it because she loved her teammates and felt obligated to carry the load for them. Have I coached better shooters? Oh yeah. Better ball handlers and passers? Without a doubt. But I've never coached a kid I had more faith in.

Gerald Davis: How was that faith fostered in Kaitlin?

Joe Gugliero: My faith in Kaitlin grew in two ways; through my observation of her work ethic and enormous ability to concentrate and focus on the task at hand and the mutual respect and admiration that grew out of our relationship. Again, it may seem odd to some, but I would often give Kaitlin the ball in situations that other players, on paper, may have been more equipped to handle from a physical standpoint. I just had a high degree of confidence that the sheer weight of her will was enough to get the job done. That instinct proved to be right more often than not.

3-POINTERS

Ephesians 2:8 (KJV) – For by grace are ye saved through faith; and not of yourselves: it is the gift of God.

Acts 16:31 – And they said, Believe on the Lord Jesus Christ and thou shalt be saved, and thy house.

1 John 5:4 (KJV) – For whatsoever is born of God overcometh the world: and this is the victory that overcometh the world, even our faith.

BUZZER BEATER

Faith – like radar that sees through the fog – is the reality of things at a distance that the human eye cannot see.
                                        - Corrie Ten Boom

POST-GAME NOTES

....
....
....
....
....
....

JOBS ... *work; employment*

Read: Mathew 9:9-12

Key Verse: Mathew 9:9 – *As Jesus was going on down the road, he saw a tax collector, Matthew, sitting at a tax collection booth. "Come and be my disciple," Jesus said to him, and Matthew jumped up and went along with him.*

Whenever you leave one coaching job for another, you want to do it for all the right reasons. As with anything in life, doing something just because you can doesn't make it right. I have seen on many occasions where coaches have left one program for another without counting the cost. What do I mean by that? First, certain questions must be asked. Is the present job a good situation for you and your family? Do you have a good working relationship with the administration? Were promises made to recruited players and their parents? Money cannot be the sole factor in changing jobs. I understand that some contracts are just too good to be true. Nonetheless, money still shouldn't be the number one reason in the pecking order.

Money was never an issue for Matthew when he made his career change. Prior to becoming one of the twelve disciples, Matthew worked as a tax collector and business was good. Therefore, when he decided to follow Jesus, Matthew did so based on the honor and privilege of being asked by the King of the universe. In the common vernacular of today, the decision was a "no brainier" – either follow Jesus or collect taxes.

Changing jobs is never an easy decision. That's why the most important thing to be done before you weigh the pros and cons of your decision is to pray. What is God saying to you about a potential job move? It's such an important life decision that God shouldn't be left out of the equation. Always remember that God wants the very best for you. If that job is for you, he will make the path accessible. No barrier or stumbling block will defer His perfect will for your life.

THE COACHES' CORNER

QUESTION AND ANSWER SESSION FEATURING:

Andy Stampfel, Head Men's Basketball Coach, The City College of New York, NY

Gerald Davis: When I'm coaching basketball I really don't consider it a job. What are some reasons why you love your job?

Andy Stampfel: I love coaching because I love sports and I love to teach. I found an affinity and passion for coaching when I started out coaching CYO. It was great to teach those kids the game, watch them learn, and watch them get better. It feeds the creative side in me as well: creating better players, better people, better teams. You also hope that your ideology and your teaching transforms into a winning machine. That's the other thing: coaching feeds my competitive appetite and allows me to stay involved in sports/athletics.

3-POINTERS

Matthew 25:21 (KJV) – His Lord said unto him, well done, thou good and faithful servant: thou hast been faithful over a few things, I will make thee ruler over many things: enter thou into the joy of thy Lord.

1 Corinthians 15:58 (KJV) – Therefore, my beloved brethren, be ye steadfast, unmovable, always abounding in the work of the Lord, for as much as ye know that your labour is not in vain in the Lord.

2 Chronicles 15:7 – But as for you, be strong; don't be discouraged, for your work has a reward.

BUZZER BEATER

I studied the lives of great men and famous women, and I found that the men and women who got to the top were those

who did the jobs they had in hand, with everything they had
of energy and enthusiasm and hard work.

- Harry S. Truman

POST-GAME NOTES

....
....
....
....
....
....
....

ORGANIZATION ... *a group of persons united for the same*
purpose

Read: Exodus 18:1-27

Key Verse: Exodus 18:18 – *You're going to wear yourself out
– and if you do, what will happen to the people?*

Moses was an excellent leader. He understood the necessity of
having a plan and being organized. However, he was working himself
to a pulp. The people who were under his charge were too numerous
to count. There were individuals who needed attitude adjustments
and personality overhauls. There were also those who believed that
the world owed them something. Moses' daily life challenges were
becoming like a pebble in a shoe – just plain annoying!

Jethro, who was Moses' father-in-law, witnessed firsthand how
Moses was struggling with the complaining Israelites. He understood the heavy burdens of being a leader and leading others was
starting to affect Moses physically. So he suggested that the workload be delegated among capable, godly, and honest men. The plan
was to divide the people into groups where appointed judges would
be responsible to hear the problems and complaints of the people.

The importance of order and organization can't be overstated. When Moses followed through on Jethro's suggestion, it definitely eased his workload. Organization can change most negatives into positives – therefore, determine to have "a place for everything and place everything in its place."

It starts with having a plan, and that plan shouldn't just be in your head. Your plan cannot be a secret. Put your plan on paper and voice it audibly. When your goal or vision is written down, it reminds you of your commitment to yourself and your team. You can only be committed to what you believe.

As coaches, our profession sometimes doesn't allow us to complete all things that must be done during the course of one day. The job can become rather time-consuming and even frustrating on some days. If you are like me, you want to get everything done that's on your "To do" list. But keep in mind: before your list can be completed, you must be organized, including your travel itineraries, daily practice plans, and season schedules. The lists can be endless, but the work must be done if you want to be a top-notch program. Some schools are fortunate enough to have secretaries, administrators, or assistants to help out the head coach, but the majority of small schools don't.

THE COACHES' CORNER

QUESTION AND ANSWER SESSION FEATURING:

Pat Torney, Head Varsity Boy's Baseball and Head Varsity Basketball Coach, Newtown High School, Queens, NY

Gerald Davis: When you're in the midst of a chaotic or stressful situation, what would your players say about you?

Pat Torney: I would hope they would say I am calm, cool, and collected. For instance, if we were down at the end of a game and I called a timeout, the first thing I would say is, "We are in this game; let's calm down and execute." Then I would go over what we specifically need to do.

Gerald Davis: Most coaches are unrelenting when it comes to structure and order. What really gets you upset when something is not in place?

Pat Torney: I get particularly frustrated when veteran players make the same mistakes over and over, or if the veterans don't recognize certain offensive or defensive sets the other team uses. I have much more patience for rookies, but I expect a lot more from the veterans.

3-POINTERS

Ecclesiastes 3:1 (NKJV) – *To everything there is a season, a time for every purpose under heaven.*

Proverbs 10:4 (KJV) – *Idle hands make one poor, but diligent hands bring riches.*

1 Thessalonians 4:7 (MSG) – *God hasn't invited us into a disorderly, unkempt life but into something holy and beautiful – as beautiful on the inside as the outside.*

BUZZER BEATER

One step and then another and the longest walk is ended. One stitch and then another, and the longest rend is mended. One brick upon another and the tallest wall is made. One flake and then another, and the deepest snow is laid.

- Anonymous

POST-GAME NOTES

....
....
....
....
....
....

POWER ... *the ability to do or act*

Read: Judges 8:28-35

Key Verse: Judges 9:5 – *He took them to his father's home at Ophrah and there, upon one stone, they slaughtered all seventy of his half-brothers, except for the youngest, Jotham, who escaped and hid.*

Blessed is the man who earns a living doing what he enjoys doing. If you would take an informal poll in an average business office, I'm sure you would find that the majority of the employees are not happy with their present position or their work environment. Then take a poll of full-time basketball coaches. I'm sure that the numbers will reflect much greater job satisfaction, and while the pressure of winning is probably more prevalent in a high profile program, the probability is high that you could *not* persuade a coach to switch jobs with an accountant, for instance (nothing against accountants). However, built into any coaching job is a certain amount of day-to-day pressure, responsibility, and power.

Power can be addictive if it is not gauged with a level head. Otherwise it will lead you down a destructive path. It happened to Abimelech, who became the King of Israel after the death of his father Gideon. Nevertheless, his rise to the throne was not the result of a natural progression in his responsibilities. Abimelech played a major part in killing seventy of his half-brothers. It was his thirst for power that eventually led to his downfall.

THE COACHES' CORNER

QUESTION AND ANSWER SESSION FEATURING:

Robert Mitchell, Girl's Basketball Coach and Instructor, Long Island, NY

Gerald Davis: Some people don't know how to use power. What are some common mistakes of a young head coach?

Robert Mitchell: Young head coaches make the common mistake of not adjusting their system to the players they have on their roster, thus forcing players to play out of their element. Another mistake is not trusting their staff and thinking that every decision and action has to come from themselves as head coach. Another abuse of their "power" is thinking that the harder they work their team, the greater the results will be. To an extent this is true, but most young coaches (and even a few older ones as well) will over-condition their teams to the point that the players have nothing to give during games. Recognizing this fine line is the difference between winning and losing games, not to mention earning your players' respect.

3-POINTERS

2 Timothy 1:7 (KJV) – For God hath not given us the spirit of fear; but of power, and love, and of a sound mind.

Luke 10:19 (KJV) – Behold, I give unto you power to tread on serpents and scorpions, and over all the power of the enemy: and nothing shall by any means hurt you.

Acts 1:8 (KJV) – But ye shall receive power, after that the Holy Ghost is come upon you.

BUZZER BEATER

Those people who are uncomfortable in themselves are disagreeable to others.

- William Hazlitt

POST-GAME NOTES

....
....
....
....
....

.... ⁄
....

REPLACEMENTS ... *something or someone that replaces*

Read: 1 Kings 19:19-21

Key Verse: 2 Kings 8:5 – *And Gehazi was telling the King about the time when Elisha brought a little boy back to life. At that very moment, the mother of the boy walked in!*

A strong bench is one of the marks of a good team. It is great when a coach can go deep into his substitution pattern and not lose a beat. Normally, however, when replacements are inserted into the game, the talent level may not be the equal of the first team. Now that doesn't mean that those replacement players cannot contribute anything positive to the program. Each member has some quality, skill, or attributes to offer. If they didn't, I'm sure they wouldn't be on the team in the first place. Sometimes coaches have the tendency to forget the "second stringers." Therefore, it's very important to teach everyone on the same level. Everyone must be able to contribute "in a pinch" when they're called on to do so. Some players may be better playing offensively than defensively. Some may bring the type of fiery attitude and personality that's needed – when it's needed!

The composition of a real team is when everyone knows his or her role and then fulfills it to the best of his or her abilities. It's the team that benefits most when each role is carried out.

Elisha was a team player in his own right. He is a great example of someone fulfilling a role, first as an apprentice and then as someone who eventually replaced his mentor as the prophet of Israel. He patiently learned his craft and observed from someone (Elijah) who had experience. Elisha didn't complain to God and say that he was better equipped than Elijah to be the head prophet. He performed every task with excellence, regardless of how minimal or pointless it may have seemed. He didn't pout over the fact that he wasn't in the forefront. Elisha understood that being a servant was of paramount importance to his becoming successful in the future.

It is, however, the responsibility of the servant/replacement/ sub to be ready when it's their time to shine! Not only was Elisha successful; he also exceeded any and all expectations. It was through God's intervention that he performed four more miracles than his mentor had done. Are your replacements ready?

THE COACHES' CORNER

QUESTION AND ANSWER SESSION FEATURING:

Mike Eisenberg, Head Varsity Girl's Basketball Coach, Francis Lewis H. S., Queens, NY

Gerald Davis: What is your normal substitution pattern during the course of a game?

Mike Eisenberg: Many different circumstances dictate my patterns. The most common ones are:

1. **Foul trouble**
2. **Match ups.** Size is usually a factor. Are my players big enough, strong enough, and quick enough to play the opponent?
3. **Game strategy.** Throughout the years we have been blessed to have some very versatile teams both offensively and defensively. Therefore, *how* we are being played (zone or man to man) will also determine *who* plays, because some players excel or fail based on the defensive coverage.
4. **Quality of the opponent.** If we are winning big, I will substitute early, use more players than usual, or play different combinations. These situations also give me an opportunity to experiment by playing starters and subs a little more than I usually would do. If the experiment and match-ups work, I will "file it in my memory bank" as an effective strategy to use in the future.

Gerald Davis: Are roles clearly defined on your teams?

Mike Eisenberg: I like to use the word "expectation" instead of the word "role." A role sometimes limits the player to do certain things well but not others; for instance, telling them, "Your role is to rebound and play defense." I'm sure that coaches have heard this quote on many different occasions. Does this mean you shouldn't score, or don't look to score, or don't practice shooting? Of course not, but players will interpret it that way, especially if expectations are not fully explained.

My players know their expectations. Guards in general need to dictate tempo, because we as a team like to "run" and usually there are better ball handlers and distributors. From year to year our bigs may be asked to do more than rebound and play defense. They could be our primary scorer. Therefore, once again, the coaches' expectations must be clear for the individual as well as for the team.

Expectations are not only meant for what players should do, but also what they should not do. That is, players who cannot shoot the 3 will not shoot one for us until they prove capable of doing so. The same goes for players who want to lead fast breaks but who shouldn't.

Gerald Davis: What do you tell the players who do not get a chance to play often?

Mike Eisenberg: I always talk to them as much as possible before, during, and after practice. I try to make them feel important. Some coaches only converse with the "stars" or starters. I will also stress the importance of practice, as well as practicing with the desire to get better. I do this while reminding them that they are only an injury, illness, ineligible player, or foul trouble away from playing meaningful minutes. Plus, starters shouldn't be allowed to become too comfortable, because they still have to practice hard to earn their playing time.

I will also press upon them to push the starters in practice because doing so is the only way we can get better as a team. And, finally, I make it a point to compliment these players as much as possible, usually in front of the team for everyone to hear. This motivates the kids who don't play often. Finally, I can remember many games where their practice contributions lead to many wins.

3-POINTERS

Genesis 22:13 (NASB) – *Then Abraham raised his eyes and looked, and behold, behind him a ram caught in the thicket by his horns; and Abraham went and took the ram, and offered him up for a burnt offering in the place of his son.*

1 Corinthians 6:7 (KJV) – *For even Christ our Passover is sacrificed for us.*

Ephesians 5:2 (KJV) – *And walk in love, as Christ also hath loved us, and hath given himself for us an offering and a sacrifice to God for a sweet smelling savor.*

BUZZER BEATER

Learn to see in another's calamity the ills which you should avoid.

- Publius Syrus

POST-GAME NOTES

....
....
....
....
....
....
....

SCOUT/SCOUTING ... *a person sent to find out what the is doing*

Read: Numbers 13:17-32

Key Verse: Numbers 13:30 – *But Caleb reassured the people as they stood before Moses. "Let us go up at once and possess it," he said, "For we are well able to conquer it!"*

Scouting for new players today can be very detail oriented. Everything is broken down offensively and defensively so that any and every advantage can be gained. In many cases it can mean the difference between winning and losing. Scouting doesn't guarantee victory, but if finding the best player can garner even the slightest advantage for your team, it's worth it. Advance scouting was a job function long before NBA organizations started sending personnel to games in order to provide detailed notes, plays, and player assignments about their next opponent.

It was normal practice for kings to send spies into occupied or unoccupied lands to determine the vulnerability of their inhabitants or their ability to cultivate produce. In Numbers 13, it describes how Moses did just that; he sent out 12 spies to explore the land of Canaan. They were given instructions to assess the land for its fertility, for the strength of its armies, and to bring back samples of what crops and plants flourished there. Now here is where the story gets tricky. *Ten* spies gave reports of failure and doom, but *two* gave reports of optimism and victory. So, the leaders were faced with a dilemma – who should they believe? Well, the choice was not as difficult as we might think. Before the children of Israel had even set foot outside of Egypt, their future and destiny had already been secured. The blessings of the Lord were theirs for the taking, but their wavering faith and disobedience would not allow them to possess the land.

Have you ever scouted a game or sent an assistant who returned from a scout, and the reports told you that you had absolutely no chance "on paper" to win? Does that mean you mail in the loss? No! You still need to prepare mentally and practice wholeheartedly without being hindered by doubt or fear. A coach cannot allow his players to see defeat or despair in his eyes. Regardless of the circumstances don't ever lose your faith!

THE COACHES' CORNER

QUESTION AND ANSWER SESSION FEATURING:

Renee Bostic, Head Women's Basketball Coach, Robert Morris College, Chicago

… and …

Brad Oringer, Assistant Men's Basketball Coach, The City College of New York, NY, NY

Gerald Davis: What is your philosophy when it comes to taking away your opponent's best player?

Renee Bostic: My philosophy on taking away my opponent's best player is to apply pressure. You need to apply ball pressure at all times. You want to make it as difficult as possible for your opponent's best player to get the ball. There will also be other situations when we will apply double teams.

Brad Oringer: Quite simply – no touches; we will do whatever we can to deny him the ball all over the court.

Gerald Davis: What is easier for you to prepare for – a team with better offensive skills, or a team with better defensive skills?

Renee Bostic: Neither. My teams are defensive minded, so we are always going to apply lots of pressure. By utilizing constant pressure we are usually dictating tempo, thus making most teams play the style that we want to play.

Brad Oringer: It's easier to prepare for a better offensive team if you average 69 points per game, but it's a rather difficult task to get 80 against a solid defense.

3-POINTERS

Numbers 13:30 (KJV) – And Caleb stilled the people before Moses, and said, Let us go up at once and possess it; for we are well able to overcome it.

Numbers 14:7 (KJV) – *And they spake unto all the company of the children of Israel, saying, the land, which we passed through to search it, is an exceeding good land.*

Numbers 13:1-2 (KJV) – *And the Lord spake unto Moses saying, send thou men, that they may search the land of Canaan, which I give unto the children of Israel: of every tribe of their fathers shall ye send a man, everyone a ruler among them.*

BUZZER BEATER

He who labors diligently need never despair, for all things are accomplished by diligence and labor.

- Menander

POST-GAME NOTES

....
....
....
....
....
....
....

STRATEGY ... *a careful plan or method; the art of devising plans toward achieving a goal*

Read: Judges 6:33-40; 7:1-25

Key Verse: Judges 7:7 – *"I'll conquer the Midianites with these three hundred!" the Lord told Gideon. "Send all the others home!"*

God is the ultimate strategist, and He has given His children the blueprint for success: His Word. It's our responsibility to be committed and obedient, and to design a life of order from His blueprint. As believers in Christ, God wants us to be administratively astute, because God is a God of order. I have been taught, "If you fail to plan, you plan to fail." Whoever penned that principle was right on the money, and any coach who tries to manage his team in a haphazard, unorganized manner will only lead his program to disarray and ultimate failure instead of success.

In our business, winning is usually the barometer that determines success. (That shouldn't necessarily be the case, but that's a topic for another day). As coaches, we know that wanting to win is one thing, but it's also crucial to keep in mind that most roads to victory start with having a plan. A strategy must be in place for success to become a reality. "Things don't just happen; they happen just the way you planned them."

Gideon was chosen by God to perform a task. God needed him to lead an army against Midian and Amalek. They were neighboring nations near Israel. However, Gideon wasn't very confident in his abilities, so he asked God to give him some proof that he was the right man for the job (Read Judges 6:33-40). Not only did he find out that God was with him, but he also realized a strategy was already in place for their guaranteed victory. The average coach would not necessarily have the odds that Gideon was presented with: 300 warriors versus thousands. Like Gideon, the coach who has faith and a strategy can overcome any obstacle.

THE COACHES' CORNER

QUESTION AND ANSWER SESSION FEATURING:

Robert Mitchell, Girl's Basketball Coach, AAU H. S.

Gerald Davis: What game planning was beneficial to you and your team during a closely contested game?

Robert Mitchell: From a defensive standpoint, we game plan the types of defense we want to play if we are behind or ahead in a close game. If we are ahead we play straight up person to person. If they have good outside shooters, we put the onus on each perimeter defender to play it "straight," with no help, and the on-the-ball defender must contain her man and not allow dribble penetration and kick-outs. On offense, if there are less than two minutes to play and we hold a lead of at least 5 points, we will run a "wheel" offense to force our opponents to foul and put us in a 1-1 situation. If we are behind, we run our "urgency" offense, designed to get off quick shots and score quickly.

Gerald Davis: Suppose you just made a coaching decision that got you a win. How does that make you feel?

Robert Mitchell: Coaching decisions made during the heat of the battle are what we are there to do. Like chess, we are constantly making moves that will pay dividends later in a contest that will ultimately lead to success. Understanding your players' capabilities and their ability to execute your agreed upon strategies is what leads to success more often than not. Changing defenses, player combinations, and chemistry recognizing your opponent's weaknesses and exploiting them mean nothing if you don't have the players. Making a decision that helps your team earn a victory is self-gratifying, as long as you share the joy with all involved.

3-POINTERS

James 4:17 (NASB) – Therefore, to one who knows the right thing to do and does not do it, to him it is sin.

Ecclesiastes 9:16 (NIV) – Wisdom is better than strength.

John 14:2-3 (KJV) – In my Father's house are many mansions: if it were not so, I would have told you, I go to prepare a place for you. And if I go and prepare a place for you, I will come again, and receive you unto myself; that where I am, there ye may be also.

BUZZER BEATER

Genius is the ability to reduce the complicated to the simple.

- C. W. Ceram

POST-GAME NOTES

....
....
....
....
....
....
....

TEAMWORK ... *joint action by a number of people to make the work of the group successful and effective*

Read: Exodus 4:1-17

Key Verse: Exodus 4:16 – *He will be your spokesman to the people. And you will be as God to him, telling him what to say.*

I'm sure when you think of Moses, you think of him as a strong, determined and righteous individual. But just like us today, there are days when we doubt ourselves and insecurities within us arise. When Moses was instructed by God to speak to Pharaoh and the Egyptian leaders regarding Israel's captivity, fear began to engulf him like a pair of vice grips. "And excuse after excuse flowed like a river" (v.10). While Moses said he had a speech impediment and wouldn't be able to get the message across, God knew he could. So God had a plan and added to the team. God called Moses' brother Aaron to be the spokesman. Knowing your personal is vital in obtaining positive results.

Within any framework of a team, there will be players who possess different gifts and abilities. Some will be better at offense, while some may excel on the defensive end. As coaches, it is our job that we mix those ingredients and assemble them into an adhesive group.

THE COACHES' CORNER

"Teamwork – The Sum of Many Parts"

By **Ed Nixon**, Former H. S. Basketball Coach, Mississippi

Teamwork is made up of many different players who are playing different positions, not just one player. If the post player says to the point guard, "I am not part of the team because I don't handle the ball all the time," does that make the post player any a less part of the team? And what if the wing player says, "I am not part of the team because I have to wait for someone to throw me the ball before I can do anything." Does that make the wing any less a part of the team? And, what if the assistant coach said, "Because I'm not the head coach, I'm not very important to the team." Does that make the assistant coach less important? What about the team manager who says, "I don't ever get to play. I'm not important at all." Does that make the manager not needed? Now, suppose the whole team was made up of point guards; who would get the rebounds underneath the goal? Or suppose the whole team was made up of post players; who would handle the ball and set up the offenses? You see, God has made each player special. And each player is different so that the team can be complete.

No one person in an athletic program can ever say to another person, "I don't need you." Even those people who are the "stars" must realize that, if it were not for those who are the "regular" players, and if not for the substitutes and support people who may never get to play in the games (statisticians, scorekeepers, managers, etc.), the "stars" would never even be in a position to be "stars." When all people realize their value to the team because of their role on the team, there is happiness among the players and all involved in the program. The result of this kind of thinking among the team members is that everyone tends to care for one another, regardless of their role on the team. Therefore, if one player suffers, all players suffer with that player. If one player is honored, all players are honored with that player and are glad for the player, the team, and the program. A win involves all members of the program, regardless of how poorly someone may have performed, and thus a win should be enjoyed by all. A loss also involves all members of the program and should be taken in such a way as to determine what everyone can do to make improvements so that victory is gained next time.

QUESTION AND ANSWER SESSION FEATURING:

Seth Goodman, Head Women's Basketball Coach, Monroe College, Bronx, NY

... and ...

Andy Stampfel, CCNY, NY

Gerald Davis: Which one of your teams has clearly evoked the spirit of teamwork?

Seth Goodman: My team two years ago during the 2004-2005 season comes to mind – when we lost in the national championship game. We were 33-1 going in and we lost by 4. That year we played many close games, and even though we had a superstar, every player on that team made a play to help win us a game over the course of the season. The girls all respected each other and played for each other. You could tell the love and respect they had for one another by their reaction after losing: they all said in their own way that they wish they could have won, but for each other, not for themselves.

Andy Stampfel: The 2002-2003 CUNY Championship team was one that evoked the spirit of teamwork. We had two seniors, two sophomores, and a freshman center start on that team. The first three players off the bench were all freshmen ... and we won the CUNY Championship. The two seniors were great players who made great play in order for us to win. But the underclassmen all knew their roles, played well in those roles, and everything just clicked perfectly for that team.

Gerald Davis: What negative effect has occurred when team-work wasn't demonstrated?

Andy Stampfel: It has been my experience, at our level, that when someone goes off on their own and gets away from our stuff, the team shuts down and gets confused. They look at each other as if to say, "Hey, he shouldn't be doing that," and then we have nothing. The other guys don't know what their roles have now become and/ or where they should go or what they should do.

Seth Goodman: My 2003-2004 team, probably my most talented team to date. We ended up 25-9. (We shouldn't have lost 9.) We won the region and made it to the nationals. The first half of the national quarterfinals I subbed out my leading scorer with 3:30 to go in the first half; we were down by 3 points. She took off her shoes in disgust and I didn't allow her to play after halftime. We lost the game by 26 points when we were heavily favored to win. We lost the next night by 2 to a team that was not very good. We ended up 7th in an 8-team tournament. We never recovered from that sneaker-gate incident.

Gerald Davis: Why do coaches place such a heavy emphasis on teamwork?

Andy Stampfel: Teamwork is vital, in my opinion, because basketball is 5 vs. 5. If you want to play a sport where you do it all on your own, play tennis. College basketball is completely different than the pros. The "pros" showcase their best players and their talent by having illegal defenses, thus making it easier for a player to go one-on-one all the time, such as what you see Kobe Bryant doing. By rule or by definition, you can't play that style in the college game and be successful. The game is a beautiful game to watch when all five guys are touching and moving the ball. The game is also a beautiful game to play when all five guys are passing and moving as a team. The problem is that all the players have been taught to play one-on-one. Their mentality is *I have the ball, so I have to do something with it*. The rest of the guys just watch, because they aren't taught how to move without the ball. Then they watch all of this played on the "professional" level, one guy going one-on-one with another with everyone else just standing around. So, they think that is how the game is played.

3-POINTERS

Ecclesiastes 4:9-10, 12 (NASB) – *Two are better than one because they have a good return for their labor. For if either of them falls, the one will lift up his companion. But woe to the one who falls when there is not another to lift him up. And if one can overpower him who is alone, two can resist him. A cord of three strands is not quickly torn apart.*

Hebrews 10:25 (NASB) – *Not forsaking our own assembling together, as is the habit of some, but encouraging one another; and all the more, as you see the day drawing near.*

Proverbs 27:17 (NASB) – *Iron sharpens iron, so one man sharpens another.*

BUZZER BEATER

Everything that lives, lives not alone nor for itself.

-William Blake

POST-GAME NOTES

....
....
....
....
....
....
....

3rd QUARTER:

Passing … it's better to give than to receive

An assist is the action of a player who enables a teammate to score. As a coach it's one of the most gratifying acts to witness on the basketball court. I take great pleasure in seeing players being unselfish. When unselfish play is evident during the course of a game, it's a beautiful thing to watch. It's one thing to preach unselfish play, but it's quite another to see it on the floor. Ask any coach if they would prefer a "ball hog" who averages 25 points per game or a Jason Kidd. I'm sure the percentages would lean heavily towards J-Kidd. I just believe that Naismith created the game for everyone on the court to enjoy – not just one individual.

I'm a New York Knicks fan, and I'm especially a fan of those teams in the 70s who hardly let the ball touch the floor. It wasn't a good possession if the ball didn't touch the hands of at least three players, which in turn would lead to a lay-up, an easy post-up, or a open jumper. Those Red Holtzman-coached teams were an example of how sharing leads to good experiences.

As believers in Jesus Christ we too can make the ultimate assist in sharing the gift of Christ. While thinking within the concept of an assist, it encompasses the ideology of giving. And, Christ gave the gift of all gifts – His life! He desires that His children do not keep "the Good News" of the gospel to ourselves, but to share it. (Didn't someone share God's love with you?)

For coaches who work in schools, colleges, or universities the question of "separation of church and state" becomes an issue. When opportunities arise for sharing the gospel with others, an inner conflict of how to disseminate the good news without being overbearing, pushy, or preachy takes place, but it can be done, my friend!

I encourage any coach who allows Christ to lead and guide them, not to change their personality just to fit a certain prototype. If you have the tendency to spit fire and brimstone while coaching, be that person. Or, if you're the "sit and stay on the bench" kind of coach, be that person; but, whatever your personality dictates – just let your light shine. You are the world's light, a city on a hill glowing in the night for all to see; don't hide your light! Let it shine for all; let your good deeds glow for all to see, so that they will praise your heavenly father (Mathew 5:14-16).

A COACH'S WIFE ... *She's your rock!*

Read: 1 Samuel 25: 1-43

Key Verse: 1 Samuel 25:3 – *"His name was Nabal and his wife, a beautiful and very intelligent woman"*

Have you ever just sat down to dinner with your family when suddenly the doorbell rings? A friend of the family comes in, and you, being the neighborly and mannerly person that you are, welcome them in to share your evening meal. Well, imagine having to entertain or feed 600 men.

It was the custom during biblical times to offer that type of hospitality to any traveler who asked. While 600 is an unusually large number, Nabal (a very wealthy man) refused David's request to give his men a meal. This act was unacceptable, primarily because it was David's men who were protecting Nabal's workforce as they tended to their daily shepherding chores. This situation could have ended in bloodshed if it wasn't for the intelligent "end-around" intervention of Nabal's wife, Abigail (v. 18, 23-34).

It's not easy being a coach's wife. That's why I'm sure they are made from a different cloth. The time factor and commitment involved is very demanding on both sides of the ledger. The "To-Do" lists can be endless – there are practices, videotape sessions, recruiting telephone calls, and so on. She may not be contributing to your X's and O's, but her list can be just as grueling and long: dealing with your preparation of scouting reports for hours at a time, putting up with your sour attitude after a loss, and understanding your need for deep introspective thinking after wins. Always remember that she's your rock! Don't take her for granted. Love and appreciate her, and not only during the "off" season. Balance is the key to peace in the home and in the workplace.

THE COACHES' CORNER

"A Wife Understands"

By **Anna Nigro**, wife of Daniel Nigro, Men's Basketball Coach

It took me a while to think of how I could describe what it's like being married to a basketball coach. Then it finally came to me, after yet another never-ending day, as I lay in bed alone again, something only a coach's wife can understand.

Only a coach's wife can understand the phone ringing all hours of the night, and why he needs to speak to his assistant coach after having been with him for four hours in practice.

Only a coach's wife can understand the commitment made to all his players, their lives and personal issues.

Only a coach's wife can understand the endless calls it takes to schedule a game, trip, or tournament.

Only a coach's wife can understand the frustration behind every bad call, bad play, missed shot, foul, non-working score board, delayed call, reach, elbow … losing by one point.

Only a coach's wife can understand the frustration behind not being able to practice or a cancelled game.

Only a coach's wife can understand what "five more minutes" really means.

Only a coach's wife can hear his thoughts haunting him all hours of the night, after a game, going over and over and over every play in his mind and thinking of what he should have done differently.

Only a coach's wife can understand the true victory of a made shot, a good play, teamwork, and the efforts that are seen on the court.

Only a coach's wife understands the triumph of a good game, a win, and a championship.

Only a coach's wife can understand why he does it at all!

QUESTION AND ANSWER SESSION FEATURING:

Terri Gugliero, wife of Joe Gugliero, Women's Basketball Coach

Gerald Davis: Do you like basketball?

Terri Gugliero: I love the game. For the past ten years I've been traveling all over with my daughters to AAU tournaments. I love watching them play and I really enjoy the game.

Gerald Davis: What is the hardest thing about being a coach's wife?

Terri Gugliero: During the season I don't get to see my husband as often as I'd like. Raising kids is tough, and sometimes his absence makes it tough for the family to deal with things that come up.

Gerald Davis: If basketball weren't a part of your life, how different would it be?

Terri Gugliero: My daughter has been playing ball since second grade. Going to practices, tournaments, and games has been a major part of our lives for the past ten years. We've had some great times, gone to some great places, and met loads of great people. When my husband's teams play I go to as many games as possible. I really enjoy it, and it's a way of sharing my husband's coaching experiences. If we didn't have basketball, my husband would be home more, and he'd probably be driving me nuts in the process. He's the kind of guy that has to keep busy. He's not a home project guy and does not like "chores." If it wasn't ball, it would be something else and perhaps something that would not interest me the way basketball does. So while ball does take him away from me, it also gives me something I can share with him.

3-POINTERS

Proverbs 31:10 (NASB) – *An excellent wife, who can find? For her worth is far above jewels.*

Genesis 2:22-24 (NASB) – *And the Lord God fashioned into a woman the rib which he had taken from the man, and brought her to the man. And the man said, "This is now bone of my bones, and flesh of my flesh; she shall be called Woman, because she was taken out of Man." For this cause a man shall leave his father and his mother, and shall cleave to his wife; and they shall become one flesh.*

Proverbs 12:4 (NIV) – *A wife of noble character is her husband's crown, but a disgraceful wife is like decay in his bones.*

BUZZER BEATER

Always meet the wife before you hire the coach.

\- Tony Demeo

POST-GAME NOTES

....
....
....
....
....
....
....

CONVICTION ... *a firm belief*

Read: Daniel 6:1-28

Key Verse: Daniel 6:22 – *"My God has sent his angel,"* he said, *"to shut the lions' mouths so that they can't touch me; for I am innocent before God, nor, sir, have I wronged you."*

Without a doubt, one of my favorite Bible personalities is Daniel. One of his traits that I admire is the pride he took while performing his duties as a counselor of kings. Daniel was also an excellent administrator, so good, in fact, that jealousy was a driving force in those who tried to get him murdered. His story is not just a fun story-telling experience for children's Sunday school lessons. His life story is a testimony of an individual who stood on the Word of God and refused to falter. When his story is being discussed, it should be done with pointed, detailed explanations of his sacrifices for truth and his undeniable spirit of conviction.

Conviction is standing when no one else wants to stand for truth and righteousness, and when your peers are doing things contrary to the Word of God. It's the inner man of a true man or woman of God that allows you to say 'no' when 'no' needs to be said. Your reputation with God is more important than your status with the sports community.

Shadrach, Meshach, and Abednego, like Daniel, were also willing to die for their convictions (Chapter 3) – and by 'die' I mean a real physical death! Isn't that what salvation is: dying to yourself so that Christ can increase? Are you willing to die to self? Do you have the courage necessary to die to the things of the world?

As a coach, it is not unusual to see unethical practices – all in the name of winning. Cheating is becoming so commonplace now that there are Web sites on how to do it "correctly." Let me tell you that a coaching position, salary, or recruit is not more important than your relationship with God. Don't be another face in the crowd; be an original! Don't be afraid to do it God's way. As a matter of fact, count it as a badge of honor! Stand firm and unmovable. Be a man or woman of conviction!

THE COACHES' CORNER

QUESTION AND ANSWER SESSION FEATURING:

Otis Henderson, Athletic Director, Christian Cultural Center, Brooklyn, New York

Gerald Davis: What is one rule you have that is unshakable while working in your role as athletic director?

Otis Henderson: To be patient. I quickly learned that working as an AD at Christian Cultural Center is a unique experience. Our timetable is different – things don't always happen when I want them to. There are plans and dreams that I have personally, but this is a ministry directed by the Lord. He guides our steps. In order to understand that, I had to really understand the nature of patience, and I had to learn to *be* patient.

When I first took the job, there were initial successes, but I did not listen to the Holy Spirit's warnings about some underlying issues. I ignored the "road signs" of danger ahead. I was so locked on my own agenda that I forgot that we are on God's timetable, not mine. Experience has taught me that God's will done His way and in His time will NEVER lack His supply and blessing. If I get ahead of that, it results in disaster.

Faith and patience obtain the promise. Patience will protect you from deception and give you a greater perspective on the proper path to take. It also helps me manage relationships with my staff. Patience helps me to develop my leadership skills and to develop other leaders.

For me, patience is KEY!

Gerald Davis: Suppose someone has just offered you your dream job, but before you sign the contract you're told that boosters regularly give players spending money – with no questions asked. How would you respond?

Otis Henderson: I would explain to the Athletic Board how honesty is the only way for me. I endeavor to live my life covered and protected by integrity. I would further explain that I could not take the job under those afore-mentioned circumstances. I would advise them that I would take the job if I were allowed to address the boosters with the Athletic Board in attendance at the meeting, and instruct the boosters to cease this practice. If the Board would also publicly denounce the practice and back me with **written** punitive steps that would be taken for violations – then I would accept the "dream job." If they could not do this, I would thank them for the offer but decline it, knowing that God has my "real" dream job waiting!

3-POINTERS

Daniel 1:8 (NASB) – But Daniel made up his mind that he would not defile himself with the king's choice food or with the wine which he drank; so he sought permission from the commander of the officials that he might not defile himself.

Daniel 3:16–17 (KJV) – Shadrach, Meshach, and Abednego, answered and said to the King, O Nebuchadnezzar, we are not careful to answer thee in this matter. If it be so, our God whom we serve is able to deliver us from the burning fiery furnace, and he will deliver us out of thine hand, O king.

Mark 11:24 (KJV) – Therefore I say unto you, what things soever ye desire, when ye pray, believe that ye receive them, and ye shall have them.

BUZZER BEATER

Faith sees the invisible, believes the incredible, and receives the impossible.

- Anonymous

POST-GAME NOTES

....
....
....

. . . .
. . . .
. . . .
. . . .

ENCOURAGEMENT ... *to give courage to; increase the hope or confidence of*

Read: Acts 9:27-31

Key Verse: Acts 9:27 – *Then Barnabas brought him to the apostles and told them how Paul had seen the Lord on the way to Damascus, what the Lord had said to him, and all about his powerful preaching in the name of Jesus.*

Who's the NBA's best 3-point shooter (Ray Allen), best assist man (Jason Kidd), best foul shooter (Dirk Nowitzki), best defender (Ben Wallace), and the Bible's best encourager? **(Barnabas)** On many occasions Barnabas was that individual on his missionary teams. He was the type of person who is a must-have on any winning team. The trips taken with Paul and Mark would not have been the same without Barnabas's encouraging words. Wouldn't you rather have someone shouting, "You can do it" instead of "You can't do anything right"?

Words are a powerful force. They can build you up or tear you down. There are instances when a coach may have to raise his voice in displeasure during a practice or game. It is very important for the coach to do so with redemptive intentions. The inner spirit of a man can easily be destroyed if criticism is done viciously.

When someone's shortcoming is evident, it would be ideal if a certain trust level had already been established with the person who's doing the reprimanding. Balance is key! Therefore, along with yelling "Bad job!" there needs to be plenty of "Nice job!" mixed in as well.

THE COACHES' CORNER

QUESTION AND ANSWER SESSION FEATURING:

Kelli Cofield, Assistant Women's Basketball Coach, Nicholls State University, LA

Gerald Davis: I understand that every coach has their own distinct way of coaching, but how does it make you feel when you see a coach humiliate or degrade a player during a game or any other situation?

Kelli Cofield: No one wants to be embarrassed or degraded in front of his or her peers. I do understand that sports can be intense, and in some situations your excitement and adrenaline causes you to act out of emotion, but I do not agree with humiliating athletes during games. I'm more of an advocate of letting the player(s) know of your displeasure on a one-on-one basis. If there are situations where you need to make an example of an athlete, I would suggest that you do that on the practice courts or in a huddle so that the spectators aren't privy to what's going on. I think that when coaches degrade and humiliate players it is a poor display of their power.

Gerald Davis: How do you dispense encouragement during intense game situations?

Kelli Cofield: My personality allows me to use sarcasm and humor to get across to my players. Oftentimes I dispense encouragement in challenging them. I sometimes present them with a challenge that I know they can surpass, but that still may be a little difficult for them. I find that it gives them a sense of accomplishment, and it usually carries over to similar situations and thus helps to raise their expectations of themselves.

Gerald Davis: Can you describe a situation or game, from when you were a player, when a coach or a player offered you positive reinforcement or encouragement?

Kelli Cofield: I was always the player that coach could yell at. In situations where many players would take it personally, I took it for what it was worth, so coach would sometimes yell at me for that reason. I learned early on to listen to *what* is said and not *how* it is said, because so much of what I took from my playing days was said at a loud octave. I'm sure there were many situations where my teammates would pat me on the back or encourage me, but the situation that sticks out in my mind is one that involved my head coach while I was playing at Stony Brook University. I'm not sure of the game situation or what team we were playing against, but I remember being in the game as a junior with four other freshmen. At that point, we weren't doing well and Coach yelled at me (privately), telling me that it was my fault. For a couple of plays I didn't understand why she would say that to me, but during a timeout it clicked and I understood completely what she was talking about. At that moment, I realized my leadership qualities, and it was encouraging that she would put me in a situation like that.

3-POINTERS

Acts 14:22 (NASB) – Strengthening the souls of the disciples, encouraging them to continue in the faith, and saying, through many tribulations we must enter the kingdom of God.

Romans 1:11-12 (NASB) – For I long to see you in order that I may impart some spiritual gift to you, that you may be established: that is, that I may be encouraged together with you while among you, each of us by the other's faith, both yours and mine.

Psalm 39:7 (NKJV) – My hope is in thee.

BUZZER BEATER

The pessimist is half-licked before he starts.
- Thomas A. Buckner

POST-GAME NOTES

....

....

....

....

....

....

....

FRIENDS ... *a person who favors and supports*

Read: 2 Samuel 12:1-13

Key Verse: 2 Samuel 12:7 – *Then Nathan said to David, "You are that rich man! The Lord God of Israel says, 'I make you king of Israel and save you from the power of Saul.'"*

It's always good as a coach when you can bounce around different ideas and strategies with a friend from the coaching fraternity. It doesn't always have to be with someone from your team or staff. Thoughts and conditions can be influenced by similar philosophies. To be honest, sometimes subordinates or those close to you are not always earnest in telling you the exact truth. They usually tell you what they think you would rather hear.

Nathan had no problem telling it like it is. Nathan, who was a prophet of God and a trusted advisor to King David, was fearless when he had to confront him. His moral character would not allow him to skirt around the truth, especially to friends, and David was a friend. David committed a few indiscretions that could not be "sugar-coated." A true friend tells you when you're sinning – even when you don't want to hear it.

There are all types of sins. The variety is endless, just like break-fast cereals. In Christ's eyes, however, all sin is sin. They are all the same. There is no big, bigger, or biggest sin. No matter what the sin or how many times the sin has been committed, Christ will forgive you and that's 100% guaranteed. We serve a compassionate and forgiving God. Nevertheless, the responsible Christian still has an obligation to God and to himself not to commit the same sin over and over again. Christ says that He will forgive us of our sins if we confess them, but don't be the individual who abuses this privilege. True repentance comes when you are truly sorry for partaking in sin and you have an honest desire not commit that particular sin or any other sin ever again.

When it comes to addressing the sin committed by a friend, family member, or player, think about this question for a moment: what type of person are you? Would you allow a friend to walk in sin just because you don't want to confront him or her? Or are you fearful that it could damage your relationship? Is it possible you are a Nathan and would try to place that individual on the path of truth and repentance? Friends understand that the truth can be confrontational. Most people don't want to hear the truth. However, if you really care for someone, the information must be made available to them whether it's good or bad.

THE COACHES' CORNER

QUESTION AND ANSWER SESSION FEATURING:

Brenda Morgan, Head Varsity Girl's Basketball Coach, Abraham Lincoln H. S., Brooklyn, NY

Gerald Davis: Who are some of your closest friends in the coaching fraternity?

Brenda Morgan: By these definitions, I do not have many friends who are coaches; most are associates. The coaches who are my friends are much older mentors, most of who have retired from coaching and originally embraced me as a student of the game because of what they saw in me. As a young coach I sought the wisdom of these very successful individuals because of their accomplishments and the relationship they cultivated with me prior to my becoming a coach. The relationships they've developed with their players and myself is something that words cannot express. I listen to former players of my friends/mentors and it sometimes brings tears to my eyes when I hear how they've touched these lives. And then I think about how God has blessed my life to do the same with those whom He has entrusted to me as a coach. There are two verses that I think really capture the essence of what this kind of friendship entails: **Proverbs 27:6** – *Faithful are the wounds of a friend,* and **John 15:15** – *Greater love hath no man than this, than a man lay down his life for his friends.*

Gerald Davis: Is it hard to maintain friendships in the coaching business?

Brenda Morgan: In all honesty, I'm not sure of how difficult it is to maintain friendships in coaching. The friends I have who are also coaches were friends before coaching was a thought in my mind; an established relationship preceded coaching. I am introduced to many coaches, and if an opportunity presents itself to work alongside them to collaborate to discuss ideas or even to plan workshops, I am very selective as to who and what I expose myself. However, I am always open to listen to ideas. I just do not like to get caught up in the nonsense. And there is a lot of craziness that comes with coaching.

To say that the coaches I know are friends is a stretch; colleagues would be a better description.

3-POINTERS

Proverbs 13:20 (NASB) – *He who walks with wise men will be wise, but the companion of fools will suffer harm.*

Proverbs 17:17 (NASB) – *A friend loves at all times, and a brother is born for adversity.*

Proverbs 18:24 (KJV) – *A man that hath friends must show himself friendly: and there is a friend that sticketh closer than a brother.*

BUZZER BEATER

Actions, not words, are the true criterion of the attachment of friends.

- George Washington

POST-GAME NOTES

....
....
....
....
....
....
....

FUNDAMENTALS ... *having to do with the foundation or basis*

Read: 1 Kings 18:16-40

Key Verse: 1 Kings 18:36 – *At the customary time for offering the evening sacrifice, Elijah walked up to the altar and prayed, "O Lord God of Abraham, Isaac, and Israel, prove today that you are the God of Israel and that am your servant; prove that I have done all this at your command."*

A flying dunk from the foul line is a spectacular play. It's a play that most fans would like to see for their price of admission. The excitement that a dunk can generate can often change the momentum of a game, although the coach understands that it's worth only two points just like a simple lay-up. The lay-up itself is one of the fundamentally basic shots in the game of basketball. Along with the jump shot, the lay-up is becoming a lost art.

Fundamentals are a very important aspect of the game. There is a difference between having a good team or a bad one. "Fundamentals! Fundamentals! Fundamentals!" is the battle cry of most coaches. Most players during practice would rather scrimmage, throw up shots, and practice the ESPN highlight dunks. Unfortunately, this is a current challenge in the landscape of basketball. As an observer in the parks, AAU tournaments, high school games,and so on, the spectacular is usually preferred, especially when it comes to selling tickets. But in most cases, it is the fundamentally sound team that will be victorious.

In the Bible, we also read about the spectacular; they're called miracles. These exploits were done by Jesus and others who allowed themselves to be used by God. Throughout the Scriptures there are many examples of miracles that demonstrated God's powerful nature. They were also used to teach, heal, provide nourishment, and even to communicate. I'm sure it was easier getting someone's attention while he or she was visualizing or experiencing a miracle. Elijah the prophet was one of those individuals that God used and spoke through. (Read 1 Kings 18:16-40).

Miracles today, however, are not the usual means by which God speaks to His children. He has chosen to speak to us more frequently through the spoken word, pastors, teachers, evangelists, and by visions or dreams. In fact, God is quite comfortable with communicating to us in ordinary ways or in little things. Whether through a book, a movie, or a television program, God can get our attention. But it's up to us to listen when He speaks. Remember, God often speaks in the still and quiet, the obvious rather than the spectacular. If you think about it, it's a lot like a lay-up instead of the dunk.

THE COACHES' CORNER

QUESTION AND ANSWER SESSION FEATURING:

Brad Oringer, Assistant Men's Basketball Coach, The City College of New York, NY

Gerald Davis: Why can't anyone shoot a jump shot consistently anymore?

Brad Oringer: Kids in general spend a lot of time "shooting around" but not really working on the "art of shooting." You must be serious about your craft and work on getting better.

Gerald Davis: Do you believe that the NBA's style of play, especially during the regular season, adds to the lack of fundamentals on the lower levels of basketball?

Brad Oringer: I don't believe that the NBA has a huge effect. However, there will always be some players who will try to emulate the moves of the NBA even though they're not skilled enough to do so.

Gerald Davis: During your practices, how much time do you spend on fundamentals?

Brad Oringer: Our practices are comprised of the following time periods:

- 30 minutes on individual skill work
- 30 – 45 minutes on individual defensive fundamentals
- 20 – 30 minutes on shooting

3-POINTERS

Matthew 7:26 – And everyone who hears these words of mine, and does not act upon them, will be like a foolish man who built his house upon the sand.

Mark 12:10 – Have you not even read this scripture: The stone which the builders rejected, this became the chief corner stone.

1 Corinthians 10:11 – According to the grace of God which was given to me, as a wise master builder I laid a foundation, and another is building upon it. But let each man be careful how he builds upon it. For no man can lay a foundation other than the one which is laid, which is Jesus Christ.

BUZZER BEATER

Success is simple. Do what's right, the right way, at the right time.

- Arnold Glasow

POST-GAME NOTES

....

....

....

....

....

....

....

FUN/LAUGHTER ... *merry play; amusement, joking; the action of laughing*

Read: Genesis 17:1-27

Key Verse: Genesis 17:19 – *"No," God replied, "that isn't what I said. Sarah shall bear you a son; and you are to name him Isaac ('Laughter'), and I will sign my covenant with him forever, and with his descendants."*

The name 'Isaac', which means laughter, must have conjured up many thoughts of blessings, laughter, and joy for Abraham and Sarah. (Naming children was a serious matter in those days.) The name of a child usually depicted the characteristics or circumstances surrounding the unborn child.

Imagine being a senior citizen and the doctor tells you that you're going to be a dad. Well, that's what happened to Abraham and Sarah. It was something they had both wanted for the longest time. However, when God told them they were going to become parents, Abraham was 99 years old and Sarah was 89 years old. Their emotions at this time must have been unexplainable, even though people lived much longer thousands of years ago. I'm sure even for them, playing a game of catch would be very difficult, especially at 110 years of age! As you read the story of Abraham and Sarah, you will see that prayer does work. Also, God is a keeper of his word and promises. He has a sense of humor, too!

142

It was also necessary for Isaac, the miracle baby, to be born, because of the covenant that God had established with Abraham. Isaac was the first descendant in fulfillment of those promises to Abraham. (Read Genesis 17:1.)

As coaches, while our job is to discipline, correct, and instruct, the game of basketball should also be fun. Games and practices shouldn't always be a "boot camp." Place yourselves in the sneakers of your players. Imagine what it feels like to be on the receiving end of yelling, screaming, and verbal explosions for two to three hours a day, five to six days a week. You don't want your players to get to the point of possibly tuning you out. The good coaches know how and when to pick and choose the times when a tongue-lashing is needed. It's okay for some levity, smiles, and laughter to be mixed in with sharp barks and mini "tirades." Always remember, **balance is the key to life**.

Do you think Abraham and Sarah enjoyed a good laugh? In the end, their ages weren't really a factor. They accepted Isaac, their gift from God, with open arms. Coach, you too can smile and have a good time – it's in your contract.

THE COACHES' CORNER

"Laughter Never Hurts"

By **Gary Smith**, Men's/Women's Basketball Coach and Boy's H. S. and College Administrator

Every coach, administrator, fan, parent, and player loves to win. Unfortunately, some coaches and programs are solely evaluated on winning and winning alone. It saddens me when I see this mentality, especially on the high school level. My coaching philosophy was never really to emphasize winning. Winning was always a by-product of having fun, learning, and understanding all the important experiences along the way.

In 1987, my women's team at City College won the ECAC Championship. In that game, with about one minute remaining, the opposing coach's frustration with losing so overwhelmed him that he threw a punch at an official. Do you think he was having fun? Winning was so important to him that it destroyed any lasting good memories for his team, and it quite possibly placed a negative stigma on his coaching career.

Here are some suggestions that have worked for my teams and for me in establishing a fun and good working and learning environment:

- Don't let winning games control your every thought as a coach.
- Develop your interpersonal skills.
- Develop a coaching environment where your players understand who is in charge. However, they should also know that they can come to you for anything.

I have had numerous success stories of athletes who it would've been easy to bet against their making it, and yet they beat the odds. What can be more gratifying than to have former athletes tell you that you're one of the reasons for their success? Keep on helping student-athletes. Continue to give them a reason for coming to the gym.

QUESTION AND ANSWER SESSION FEATURING:

Karina Jorge, Assistant Women's Volleyball Coach, Sport Information Director, The City College of New York, NY

... and ...

Brad Oringer, Assistant Men's Basketball Coach, The City College of New York, NY

Gerald Davis: What makes the game of basketball fun for you?

Brad Oringer: Seeing kids perform in games what you've taught them in practice is music to a coach's ear – no, make that *beautiful* music!

Gerald Davis: Many coaches encourage their players to perform at a high standard, but to have *fun* while doing it. What have you or head coaches whom you have worked for done to accomplish this?

Karina Jorge: Encouraging team unity, not only on the court but off it as well, has been something that we have worked into our daily routines. We also make sure our players know each other well and interact with each other off the court.

3-POINTERS

Psalm 16:11 (KJV) – Thou wilt shew me the path of life: in thy presence is fullness of joy; at thy right hand there are pleasures for evermore.

Psalm 144:15 (KJV) – Happy is that people, that is in such a case; yea, happy is that people, whose God is the Lord.

Proverbs 29:18 – Where there is no vision, the people perish: but he that keepeth the law, happy is he.

BUZZER BEATER

Life is long; don't run out of fun!

- A. R. Bernard

POST-GAME NOTES

....
....
....
....
....
....
....

LOVE ... *an intense affection for another person based on personal or familial ties*

Read: 1 John 3:1-24

Key Verse: 1 John 3:23 – *And this is what God says we must do: Believe on the name of his Son Jesus Christ, and love one another.*

It would be my great pleasure to have a close relationship with all my former players long after my coaching days are over. I like to tell my players all the time that I want them to feel welcome to return with their children – so that I can tell their kids all about how great their parents were as players. This can only happen if love is fostered within the make-up of your coaching character.

It doesn't matter how rough and tough you are during practices and games: your players should know that they can come to you with any problem or situation. A level of trust, respect, and parental love is earned over time. Strive for it with all your heart! Don't feel that it will make you less of a coach. You can separate the "hard as nails taskmaster" from the "cotton-soft heart" who can love easily. That's why I don't take the position of coach and calling someone coach lightly. It's more than X's and O's; you are in a position to impact lives. Coaching can be a life-changing occupation for you and for your players.

As disciples of Christ, we are learning daily how to love – which should be like Jesus Christ himself. John, an original disciple, witnessed firsthand Christ's love for us and was inspired by God to write about his love in the Gospel of John and in the books of 1, 2, and 3 John. If I could give each reader an opportunity to write about their love for Christ, the testimonials would be endless. We couldn't begin to repay Christ for the love He shows toward us, and for His many blessings, not even if we had billions of dollars at our disposal. But even if we did, He wouldn't want it. All that Christ desires from His children is our love, not 25 or 50 percent of it, but all! Christ also desires that we love ourselves – and one another – and our enemies!

LOVE YOURSELF

How can you fulfill God's commandments of loving others without first loving yourself? Self-respect stems from loving yourself. This self-love is not smug or vain, yet it still presents an air of confidence, assurance, and sureness, which should exist in the emotional make-up of a king's kid.

LOVE ONE ANOTHER

David and Jonathan were not brothers in the natural, but they had a bond, unity, and closeness like what is normally found between brothers. Even if they weren't "blood brothers," they couldn't have been any closer. The love that existed between them continually displayed the attributes of Jesus Christ. Whenever their love for each other was tested, it withstood the test. It's one thing to declare love, but it's another to demonstrate love through deeds. When David was under heavy persecution from Jonathan's father King Saul, Jonathan's love, respect, and friendship for David never faltered.

LOVE YOUR ENEMIES

Yes, the above subtitle "Love your enemies" is not a typographical error! You probably know someone who really gets on your nerves to the point that you wish you could hate them and be justified in doing so. Well, forget that thought! You have to love that individual as if they were your natural blood brother or sister. It sounds difficult, and sometimes it is, but it is not impossible.

I'm quite sure that those Roman soldiers at Calvary must have thought Jesus was crazy. When He said, "Father, forgive them, for they know not what they do," the characteristic that was being demonstrated at the time was forgiveness. Learn how to forgive and only then will you be able to sincerely love your enemy.

For a four-letter word, LOVE sure does pack a wealth of power! As we read in John 3:16 – "For God so loved the world, that he gave his only begotten Son, that whosoever believeth in him should not perish but have everlasting life." It is this type of love that exemplifies the very character of Christ, which makes loving yourself, others, and even loving your enemies much easier, because Christ has already showed us how.

3-POINTERS

1 John 4:12 (KJV) – *Beloved, let us love one another: for love is of God; and every one that loveth is born of God, and knoweth God.*

1 John 4:16-19 (KJV) – *And we have known and believed the love that God hath to us. God is love; and he that dwelleth in love dwelleth in God, and God in him. Herein is our love made perfect, that we may have boldness in the day of judgement: because as he is, so are we in this world. There is no fear in love; but perfect love casteth out fear: because fear hath torment. He that feareth is not made perfect in love. We love him, because he first loved us.*

1 Corinthians 13:13 (NASB) – *But now abide faith, hope, love, these three; but the greatest of these is love.*

BUZZER BEATER

A true love of God must begin with a delight in His holiness.

- Jonathan Edwards

POST-GAME NOTES

···
···
···
···
···
···
···

OPENNESS ... *accessible or available*

Read: Luke 1:26-38

Key Verse: Luke 1:38 – *Mary said, "I am the Lord's servant, and I am willing to do whatever he wants."*

I learned a long time ago that not everyone who calls him- or herself a coach actually walks in that calling. That's right, coaching is and should be something you're called to do and not just something you have a passion for, because there are so many different situations that a coach must address, teach, or even experience. It is of the utmost importance for your heart to be open to the things of God and that you are an obedient and ready listener. Why? Because coaching isn't always done "by the book." There will be times when you must "think outside of the box" and develop a totally new manual, with God dictating your course.

Mary was one of those individuals who was open. She had to be open to receive the news that she would become the mother of God. That's earth-shattering news to say the least. Mary is one of the most respected and revered women in the history of the gospel. She was a woman of God who willingly submitted to the leading of the spirit of God. She withstood the whispers and the accusatory looks from others. She stood firm on the prophesied Word from God Himself, a word that trumpeted that she was the selected vessel that God wanted to use to usher in the Savior of the world. What an awesome task and responsibility, a task that would be the envy of any honorable woman who's serving the one true and living God. Are you open and **flexible** to serve God in whatever manner He sees fit?

THE COACHES' CORNER

"Openness"

By **Deirdre Moore**, Assistant Women's Basketball Coach, C. W. Post University, Greenvale, NY

As a coach, it's not always easy to get student athletes to open up to you. I have always believed that the more openness you have in a relationship the easier it is for someone to decide if they can trust you. When I was recruiting a particular player, I noticed that it was difficult for her to open up and talk about things. She came in as one of eight new players, and it seemed as if she didn't know what she could and couldn't say. She was a natural scorer, but she was being asked to run the point guard spot. Along with this position came a lot of frustration. I often talked with her about situations and ways to read the defense along with re-assuring her that she was doing a good job. However, I noticed that I wasn't really getting through to her.

Over a period of time, I began sitting with her after practices just talking to her about school, family, and things in general. Even in those conversations she would talk up to a point and then emotionally shut down. I told her that she was closing the door. This sort of became our little joke, but it was the truth. So many times whenever we talked I would remind her that she was closing the door. I told her whenever she was ready to open the door I would be there to listen. This seemed to work. What started to happen is that while she would talk, she would then say, "I know I'm closing the door again," or she would say, "I'm not ready to open that door yet."

While this was happening, she began to trust me. This helped her not to feel so frustrated in practice. She began to understand the corrections I gave her. She began to grasp concepts about running the point that I was trying to get through to her. Learning to recognize on her own when she was opening up and closing up allowed her to see the game in a different way. It made her have confidence in the things that I was teaching her; not that she was doing everything right, but she was able to differentiate the things she was doing on the court.

What I learned from this experience is that if your players can open up to you, they will trust you. If they trust you, they will try their best to do what you ask them to do. They won't want to let you down. Who doesn't want a player who is willing to run into a wall for you just because you told them to? Sometimes coaches only focus on the basketball aspect of the player, but to get that player to play for you, there must be a connection to you. I've found that having openness is one way to achieve that. Openness is both truth and honesty. If a player feels their coach is being truthful and honest with them and not playing "head games" with them, they in turn will perform.

QUESTION AND ANSWER SESSION FEATURING:

Eddie Grezensky, Head Girl's Basketball Coach, Murray Bergtraum H. S. NY, NY

... and ...

Brenda Morgan, Head Girl's Basketball Coach, Abraham Lincoln H. S., Brooklyn, NY

... and ...

Andy Stampfel, Head Men's Basketball Coach, The City College of New York, NY, NY

Gerald Davis: Do you have an "open door" policy with your players?

Brenda Morgan: Yes, I have an open-door policy with my players; they can discuss any issue they're facing with me at anytime when I'm free. However, they know that I'm a Christian, and oftentimes they don't like the answers or advice they receive from me. But they know I'm not here to judge them. Most of them understand that I have their best interests in mind. I let them know how rough the real world can be and that they really don't know it all. Sometimes they send someone else to test the waters, and I know when that's the case. My prayer is that I never become unapproachable. I hear some of the things people and coaches tell these young people, and it's sad. I just want to empower them with the correct information that will help them later in life to make informed and well thought out decisions.

> *Matthew 7:7-8 – Ask and it shall be given you; seek, and you shall find, knock and it shall be opened unto you. For every one that asketh receiveth; and he that seeketh findeth; and to him that knocketh it shall be opened.*

Andy Stampfel: My door is always open. I don't know what else to do to get these guys to come over to the office to talk and/or to help them with schoolwork or life issues. Our guys won't make the trip across the street to come and see us. This upcoming year we are going to take a page out of Jim Calhoun's book and make it mandatory for every player to stop in the office every day. We make available to them all the support we can offer. The players have to do a better job on their end. We have to teach them how to do it.

Eddie Grezensky: I try to have an open-door policy with my players. If someone has a problem, I encourage them to meet with me behind closed doors. I don't want them to **air** out their dirty laundry in front of the team.

3-POINTERS

> *Romans 5:2 (KJV) – By whom also we have access by faith into this grace wherein we stand, and rejoice in hope of the glory of God.*

> *Ephesians 2:18 (KJV) – For through him we both have access by one spirit unto the father.*

> *Ephesians 3:12 (KJV) – In whom we have boldness and access with confidence by the faith of him.*

BUZZER BEATER

Keep away from people who try to belittle your ambitions. Small people always do that, but the really great make you feel that you, too, can become great.

- Mark Twain

POST-GAME NOTES

....
....
....
....
....
....
....

PRAISE ... *saying that a thing or person is good; words that tell the worth or value of a thing or person*

Read: Psalm 101:1-8

Key Verse: Psalm 101:1 – *I will sing about your loving kindness and your justice, Lord. I will sing your praises!*

It is recorded in the Word that we are commanded to praise: "Praise the Lord! Praise God in his sanctuary; Praise him in his mighty expanse" (Psalm 150:1). Most people think of "the Coach" as the hard taskmaster. Coaching, however, is not just about yelling and screaming. While it's important to get the most out of your athletes, there is more than one way to get that accomplished. One way, which has been proved to be very successful, is by giving praise. Praising someone for their positive contributions in games or practices should be a regular part of your repertoire. Some coaches don't like to do it too often in fear that a player will get a "big head" or an inflated ego. Most coaches, however, know how to implement praise in the necessary doses, especially if it's well deserved.

When it comes to praising God, the amount of time spent doing so should never become an issue. I'm sure God has been good to you! Don't be a lackadaisical praising Christian. Some people behave as if we are doing God a favor by praising Him.

Leadership styles vary from coach to coach, but one must understand the factors involved. A good encouraging word can go a long way in building up a player's self-esteem. There can also be negative adverse effects when someone is not praised enough. The key to distributing praise is in understanding your roster and balance. Knowing the characteristics and personality of your players is also important. Certain buttons can be pushed, and if praising is one of them – praise away.

THE 4 C'S OF WHY WE PRAISE GOD

GOD'S CHARACTER

> Righteous – Isaiah 53:11
> Merciful – Hebrews 2:17

GOD'S COMPASSION

> Toward those who are poor – Matthew 8:2-4;
> Weary, and heavy laden– Mathew 11:28-30

CHRIST'S DEVINE NATURE

> Son of God – Mathew 26:63-67
> One with the Father – John 10:25-30
> Savior and Judge – 2 Corinthians 5:10

CREATED TO PRAISE HIM

Psalm 102:16-20
Deuteronomy 6:13
John 4:23

HOW WE SHOULD PRAISE

Clapping of hands – Psalm 47:1
Dancing – Ecclesiastes 3:4; Psalm 149:3
Lifting of our hands – Nehemiah 8:6; 1 Timothy 2:8
Musical Instruments – Psalm 33:1-3
Singing – Psalm 100:2; 126:2

THE COACHES' CORNER

QUESTION AND ANSWER SESSION FEATURING:

Deborah Mortley, Head Varsity Girl's Basketball Coach, Bishop Louglin Memorial H. S, Brooklyn, NY

… and …

Brenda Morgan, Head Varsity Girl's Basketball Coach, Abraham Lincoln H. S., Brooklyn, NY

Gerald Davis: Would you say that you praise more or yell more as a coach?

Deborah Mortley: This is my 19th year in coaching, and I've learned to praise more as I coach. I do still yell when I've told the players on the court countless times to execute a particular play or defense that is not being done.

Brenda Morgan: I would say I praise more at practice and in games; yelling has never been my thing. Players need to be told "what to do" – they don't need to be yelled at. If they're doing something wrong, it's because that they don't know *what* to do. I learned this from my mentors. I am an educator, and I take that to the game. *"Let another man praise you, and not your own mouth"*

Gerald Davis: Why do you believe praise is an effective tool for a coach?

Deborah Mortley: Praise is effective because players respond better to positive, constructive criticism and are willing to do more when they feel they are not being put down or embarrassed. Giving praise allows the coach a chance to calm down and think about what is being said.

Brenda Morgan: Praise is an effective tool for a coach because it notes progress, enhances learning, and it's a confidence builder. As my pastor teaches, "Long after they forget what you do, they remember how you made them feel." We're in the business of creating memories – and winning games, of course.

3-POINTERS

Psalm 7:17 (KJV) – I will praise the Lord according to his righteousness: and will sing praise to the name of the Lord most high.

Psalm 48:1 (KJV) – Great is the Lord, and greatly to be praised in the city of our God, in the mountain of his holiness.

Psalm 68:3 (KJV) – But let the righteous be glad; let them rejoice before God: yea, let them exceedingly rejoice.

BUZZER BEATER

God gave you a gift of 86,400 seconds today. Have you used one to say "thank you"?

- William A. Ward

POST-GAME NOTES

....

....

....

....

....

....

....

RESPECT ... *honor; esteem*

Read: 2 Samuel 3:1-39

Key Verse: 2 Samuel 3:31 – *"Then David said to Joab and to all those who were with him, "Go into deep mourning for Abner."*

Part of the game of basketball is "matching wits" against your coaching counterparts. It's one of the reasons why a coach coaches, while it's the players who usually decide the game on the floor. It's fun when a coach can make a subtle change or minor adjustment that could possibly determine the outcome of a game. It's the ultimate compliment and sign of respect when the opposing coach recognizes these moves – whether during post-game interviews or post-game conversations.

In the Old Testament, Abner and David fought at one time for the same team after Saul came into power. As his obsession to kill David grew stronger, Abner's loyalties sided with King Saul. But his and David's mutual respect for each other remained, regardless of the opposing uniforms they wore. This occurred because respect is earned over time. Over the years, these men had seen the good times and the bad times with each other. Thus, the mettle of a real man must come out. They both experienced that, especially during times of war.

THE COACHES' CORNER

QUESTION AND ANSWER SESSION FEATURING:

Robert Mitchell, Girl's Basketball Coach, Personal Instructor

Gerald Davis: How do you gain respect as a head coach?
Robert Mitchell: Respect must be earned. Respect is earned not by how well we know the X's and O's, but by how well we are able to communicate to our players how much they mean to us as human beings. Caring about what is happening in their lives, their homes, and at school goes a long way toward earning their respect.
Gerald Davis: When respect is lost, can it be regained?
Robert Mitchell: Like any relationship where trust is broken, respect can be regained, but you must be willing to put in the effort to make that happen. Life is about labor and reward: no labor ... no reward.

3-POINTERS

1 Peter 2:17 (NASB) – *Honor all men; love the brotherhood, fear God, honor the king.*

Proverbs 15:33 (NASB) – *The fear of the Lord is the instruction for wisdom, and before honor comes humility.*

Psalm 119:15 (KJV) – *I will meditate in thy precepts, and have respect unto thy ways.*

BUZZER BEATER

Nobody holds a good opinion of a man who has a low opinion of himself.

- Anthony Trollope

POST-GAME NOTES

....
....
....
....
....
....
....

RULES ... *statements concerning what to do and not to do; principles governing conduct and actions*

Read: Genesis 3:1-24

Key Verses: Genesis 3:2-3 – *"Of course we may eat it,"* the *woman told him. "It's only the fruit from the tree at the center of the garden that we are not to eat."*

Rules are necessary if order is regarded as a high premium in your program. I'm not an advocate of having too many rules, but the rules that I do have in place must be adhered to. Rules are also given for our protection, guidance, and instruction. Without rules, chaos will reign and a program filled with chaos will ultimately lead to its downfall.

Adam found this out on a first-hand basis. God had given him a good job (that of a zoologist) with only one rule: Do not eat of the tree of knowledge. Because of Adam and Eve's disobedience, they both suffered consequences – and it impacted mankind. One act shattered the relationship between God and man.

After Adam and Eve ate the fruit, it was Adam who was called on the carpet by God, not Eve! Even though it was Eve who first entertained the serpent's deception, God held Adam responsible for what had transpired in the Garden of Eden. Why? Because this one rule and its accompanying instructions had been given directly to Adam (Genesis 3: 9-11).

When rules and regulations are broken or when something goes wrong, your Athletic Director is not going to look at the assistants or players. He's going to seek out the person who is in charge of the team – you as the head coach. So don't play the blame game like Adam did: "But it was the woman you gave me!"

THE COACHES' CORNER

QUESTION AND ANSWER SESSION FEATURING:

Robert Mitchell, Girl's Basketball Coach, Personal Instructor

Gerald Davis: Are you a big proponent of having many rules on your teams?
Robert Mitchell: I am a big proponent of team rules. There must be structure, and having a team handbook of rules that must be followed by EVERYONE on the team is mandatory. Then there will be no gray area for interpretation if the "star" player(s) break the "TEAM" rules, because the rules apply to one and all. At the beginning of each season I have a meeting with the team members and their parents, and they must sign-off that they've received and read the handbook of rules in order to be a member of the team.
Gerald Davis: Do you consider yourself a disciplinarian?
Robert Mitchell: Every team must have discipline in order to work together as a team, and it starts from the top. While I'm not a "Coach Carter" type, I control my team through mutual respect.

3-POINTERS

2 Timothy 2:5 (NASB) – And also if anyone competes as an athlete, he does not win the prize unless he competes according to the rules.

Psalm 119:165 (NASB) – Those who love thy law have great peace, and nothing causes them to stumble.

James 1:22 (KJV) – *But be ye doers of the word, and not hearers only, deceiving your own selves.*

BUZZER BEATER

When you have a curfew, it's always your star who gets caught.

- Abe Lemons

POST-GAME NOTES

....
....
....
....
....
....
....

WORSHIP ... *to honor or reverence; to regard with great respect*

Read: John 4:21-24

Key Verses: Revelation 22:8-9 – *I, John, saw and heard all these things, and fell down to worship the angel who showed them to me; but again he said, "No, don't do anything like that. I, too, am a servant of Jesus as you are, and as your brothers the prophets are, as well as all those who heed the truth stated in this Book. Worship God alone."*

When I hear the word "worship" associated with athletes, I just cringe. There are no exploits or accomplishments in any sport that warrant worship status. Sometimes the sports community gets out of control when worship superlatives are bantered about. Worship is an action word that should only be connected with God and God alone.

CHARACTERISTICS OF A WORSHIPPER

We read in Luke 7:36-50the story of a former prostitute who understood what it meant to worship Jesus. She demonstrated sacrifice, fearlessness, and brokenness before Him.

Sacrifice: She demonstrated a total surrender to the will of God. It was her first step in attempting to live a sinless lifestyle. Her offering of worship (when she poured perfume on the feet of Jesus) was not forced but voluntary.

Fearlessness: She didn't care what people thought of her. Her only goal was to meet Him.

Brokenness: Her emotions of love were sincere and from the heart. The kisses and tears depicted her overwhelming thankfulness for being forgiven and were the result of knowing that she was in the presence of the Almighty God.

THE COACHES' CORNER

QUESTION AND ANSWER SESSION FEATURING:

Robert Mitchell, Girl's Basketball Coach, Instructor, Long Island, NY

… and …

Joe Gugliero, Women's Girl's Basketball Coach, Long Island, NY

Gerald Davis: As a coach you would prefer that no one worship you. What would be some things you wouldn't mind a player saying about you as a coach and a person?

Robert Mitchell: I would have to say the things that I want said about me are that I am a man of moral character and principle, and that I care about the development of my players as human beings, citizens, and basketball players – in that order. You reap what you sow.

Joe Gugliero: I want my players to be able to say–

- I know he cares about me as a human being first and an athlete second.
- I respect and trust him.
- When I have a problem he is one of the first people I turn to.
- He not only taught me more about the game than any other coach I've ever had, but he also taught me about life and helped me to become a better person.
- I didn't always agree with him and sometimes we did buck heads, but he was always fair and consistent.
- It's been ten years since I played my last basketball game, and Coach and I continue to share a warm and open relationship.

3-POINTERS

Psalm 95:6-7 (KJV) – *O come, let us worship and bow down: let us kneel before the Lord our maker. For he is our God; and we are the people of his pasture, and the sheep of his hand.*

Psalm 24:9-10 (KJV) – *Lift up your heads, O ye gates; even lift them up, ye everlasting doors; and the king of glory shall come in. Who is this king of glory? The Lord of hosts, he is the King of glory.*

Psalm 100:1-3 – *Make a joyful noise unto the Lord, all ye lands. Serve the Lord with gladness: come before his presence with singing. Know ye that the Lord he is God: it is he that hath made us, and not we ourselves; we are his people, and the sheep of his pasture.*

BUZZER BEATER

The unthankful heart discovers no mercies, but the thankful heart will find in every hour some heavenly blessings.

- Henry Ward Beecher

POST-GAME NOTES

....

....

....

....

....

....

....

OVERTIME:

Free throws ... knock them down

In the overtime section we will examine areas in our lives that we must actively practice in order to meet the moral standards of Jesus Christ, our model of excellence.

Shaquille O'Neal, Wilt Chamberlain, Tim Duncan – all Hall-of-Famers, but they have one thing in common: they were not the greatest shooters from the foul line. I have often watched games from the comfort of my family room and wondered aloud as to why these million-dollar athletes can't shoot at least 70% from the free-throw line. I'm sure they were instructed just like many of us wanna-be-ballers were. But for some reason, the NBA as a whole doesn't consistently shoot free throws well.

There are many factors that are involved in being a consistent shooter from the foul line, but the primary factor is practice. Now, that's not to say that these players don't or didn't practice. Some players even have personal shooting experts. But it still comes down to working hard.

Isn't it the same for the believer? There are areas in our lives that we just *have* to work on, and not just some days, but every day! Satan loves to keep believers from reaching their potential. And he will succeed, especially if we are not **praying:** "I will pray morning, noon, and night, pleading aloud with God; and he will hear and answer" (Psalm 55:17).

We also need to be **reading the word** regularly: "The copy of the laws shall be his constant companion. He must read from it every day of his life so that he will learn to respect the Lord his God by obeying all of his commands" (Deuteronomy 17:19). Also, we should be **attending a house of worship on a consistent basis:** "Let us not neglect our church meetings, as some people do, but encourage and warn each other, especially now that the day of his coming back again is drawing near" (Hebrews 10:25). And, even if we do these things on a regular basis we will fail at times, but it is imperative that we don't remain in that "state of failure."

ANGER ... *the feeling one has toward something or someone that hurts, opposes, offends, or annoys*

Read: Genesis 4:1-24

Key Verse: Genesis 4:5 – *This made Cain both dejected and very angry, and his face grew dark with fury.*

Why did Cain become so distraught and disappointed when God did not accept his sacrifice? The answer? He allowed his emotions to choose for him – and he chose wrong! The end result was murder! His emotions resulted in a multitude of problems for himself and mankind. He didn't understand that for every action there are consequences.

The Game of Life, like basketball, can also be intense and filled with emotion. Basketball, like most sports is very emotional. Depending on the level of competition and the importance of the game, coaches and players have been known at times to lose their cool." This is usually in the middle of the madness when the referee or **umpire** has missed a call. Whether they like it or not at that moment, they are the most disliked individuals on the court. When a call or decision goes against a team at a critical juncture in a game, it can be disappointing. It's one of the hardest things to do but you have to keep your composure!

The Bible says that we *will* get angry (Ephesians 4:26); however, Christ's desire is that we don't sin in the process. Remember, regardless of the venue, God wants to see how we handle adversity. Once you confer Christianity to men, the rules of the game change because someone is always watching. Don't give the fans, spectators, or opposing players the opportunity to say, "But I thought he (she) was a Christian!"

THE COACHES' CORNER

QUESTION AND ANSWER SESSION FEATURING:

Michael Krasnoff, Head Women's Basketball Coach, Old Westbury College, NY

Gerald Davis: What really gets you angry on the basketball court?

Michael Krasnoff: What gets me angry is when an official or officials don't hustle to give you the best they have. Also, their job is not to try and keep the game even as some try and do. Teams are different, some more aggressive than others, meaning fouls will never be even, nor should they be. I don't think the foul count is something that should affect the way an official calls a game. Consistency is the key.

Gerald Davis: When an official makes a bad call, what are some things you do to calm yourself down?

Michael Krasnoff: I have purposely become certified in Board 41 to make myself a better coach by learning the rules, and more than that, by learning the positioning and the mindset of officials. It's still not pleasant to deal with even if you understand what they do and why, but it's a little easier to tolerate. Being an official, I have learned how to discuss a questionable call without making an official look bad.

3-POINTERS

James 1:19-20 (NASB) – This you know, my beloved brethren. But let everyone be quick to hear, slow to speak and slow to anger; for the anger of man does not achieve the righteousness of God.

Psalm 37:8-9
(KJV) – Cease from anger, and forsake wrath: fret not thyself
in any wise to do evil. For evildoers shall be cut off: but
those that wait upon the Lord, they shall inherit the earth.

Ephesians 4:26 (KJV) – Be ye angry, and sin not: let not the
sun go down upon your wrath.

BUZZER BEATER

Anger dwells only in the bosom of fools.

- Albert Einstein

POST-GAME NOTES

....
....
....
....
....
....
....

ATTITUDE ... *a way of thinking, acting, or feeling*

Read: 2 Chronicles 14:1-15

Key Verse: 2 Chronicles 14:11 – *"O Lord," he cried out to*
God, "no one else can help us! Here we are, powerless against this
mighty army. Oh, help us, Lord our God! For we trust in you alone
to rescue us, and in your name we attack this vast horde. Don't let
mere men defeat you!

Do you have a win-at-all-cost attitude? If so, it's not the character
that Christ wants you to have as a representative of the kingdom of
God. That doesn't mean you shouldn't have a competitive nature.
You can be a winner and still display humility with a touch of class.

Jesus Christ wants you to succeed, but it must be done with dignity. A win-at-all-cost mentality means you are willing to do anything and to hurt anyone in the process (which is not very Christ like).

Asa, the King of Judah, started his reign on a positive note. Heathen altars and idols were out of the question. He was strict and impartial. His edicts would also affect the queen, his mother Maacah, who was also an idol worshiper. Then the "tide for righteousness" began to shift. He resorted to his own will instead of that of the Father. That's when he was headed for failure. He bribed King Ben-hadad of Syria with gold and silver so that he would break his alliance with King Baasha of Israel. It was King Asa who had problems with King Baasha, not Ben-hadad. Nevertheless, it was the wayward thinking and poor attitude of Asa that contributed to his downward spiral.

THE COACHES' CORNER

QUESTION AND ANSWER SESSION FEATURING:

Seth Goodman, Head Women's Basketball Coach, Monroe College, Bronx, NY

Gerald Davis: I love repeating quotes from famous personalities or authors to my players. What is one of your favorite quotes that speaks about ATTITUDE?

Seth Goodman: I don't know who first said it, but I love the quote, "You cannot sink the end of someone else's boat without sinking yours."

I also quote Proverbs 18:14: "The human spirit can endure a sick body, but who can bear it if the spirit is crushed?" **Gerald Davis:** Why is having a good attitude a must-have quality?

Seth Goodman: It is a long season with many highs and lows if you have a bad attitude, and when things are low, you will never enjoy the highs.

3-POINTERS

Titus 2:6-8 – *Likewise urge the young men to be sensible; in all things show yourself to be an example of good deeds, with purity in doctrine, dignified, sound in speech which is beyond reproach, in order that the opponent may be put to shame, having nothing bad to say about us.*

Philippians 4:8 (KJV) – *Finally, brethren, whatsoever things are true, whatsoever things are honest, whatsoever things are just, whatsoever things are pure, whatsoever things are lovely, whatsoever things are of good report; if there be any virtue, and if there be any praise, think on these things.*

Mark 9:23 (KJV) – *Jesus said unto him, if thou canst believe, all things are possible to him that believeth.*

BUZZER BEATER

Nothing can stop the man with the right mental attitude from achieving his goal; nothing on earth can help the man with the wrong mental attitude.

- W. W. Ziege

POST-GAME NOTES

....
....
....
....
....
....
....

BITTERNESS ... *pain; grief*

Read: 2 Samuel 6:1-23

Key Verse: 2 Samuel 6:16 – *But as the procession came into the city, Michal, Saul's daughter, watched from a window and saw King David leaping and dancing before the Lord; and she was filled with contempt for him.*

Bitterness can be a destructive emotion because it can eat at you like a disease from the inside out. If you're unable to cope with all of society's physical and psychological demands, those can lead you straight to a mental hospital. That's why it is imperative for your good health and mental well being to deal with it immediately if something or someone is disturbing your peace, whether it's done by talking it out with them in a calm, discreet manner or screaming into a brown paper bag when no ones else is around to see or hear you!

The bitterness that stirred within Michal contributed towards the separation between her and King David in their marriage. Some say it may have been inevitable because of her genetic bloodline, because Michal was the daughter of the wicked King Saul. One reason for her unrelenting tension and resentment was her failure to understand that man was created to worship and praise God! When she witnessed praise and worship in action from her husband in the highest order, Michal just didn't know how to handle it.

David couldn't contain his joy and happiness as he led a procession of the triumphant Israelites as they returned the Ark of the Covenant to its rightful place. The Ark was originally built to hold the tablets of the Ten Commandments. The Ark was Israel's most sacred object. For a long period of time the Ark had lain in the hands of the Philistines and then in the residence of Abinadab. David's celebration was so intense that Michal must have thought he was losing his mind. Her respect for David dimmed even further because of her lack of understanding regarding praise and worship. It's hard to imagine that such distain would form in someone's heart from watching another person praise and worship God. Nonetheless,

Michal's lack of commitment to the things of God surely contributed to her bitterness toward David. Those feelings must have been festering within her long before the Ark celebration.

It's important not to keep negative or hurtful things in your heart as a coach. You will face a boatload of situations that could allow bitterness to build up within you if you let it. Whether it's a blown call from a referee, an incorrect assignment by a player, or a TV announcer who you believe is being unfair with their commentary, a good rule of thumb is to just let it go. By this I mean let it go to the point of not even acknowledging its existence or potential problem. If it does bother you or you think that something unjust has occurred that truly needs to be dealt with, "nip it in the bud" or bitterness will bloom. Also, don't conduct yourself like a spoiled brat and tell everyone about an issue or challenge without first discussing it with the primary individual involved.

THE COACHES' CORNER

QUESTION AND ANSWER SESSION FEATURING:

Eddie Grezensky, Head Varsity Girl's Basketball Coach, Murray Bergtraum H. S., NY, NY

Gerald Davis: Can you describe your hardest loss as a coach?
Eddie Grezensky: My hardest loss as a coach is when we lose a game because of lack of effort; not when we lose to a better team.

3-POINTERS

Hebrews 12:15 (NASB) – See to it that no one comes short of the grace of God; that no root of bitterness springing up causes trouble, and by it many be defiled.

Ephesians 4:31 (KJV) – Let all bitterness, and wrath, and anger, and clamour, and evil speaking, be put away from you, with all malice.

Proverbs 17:25 (KJV) – A foolish son is a grief to his father, and bitterness to her that bare him.

BUZZER BEATER

Bitterness imprisons life; love releases it.

- Harry Emerson Fosdick

POST-GAME NOTES

....
....
....
....
....
....
....

DECEPTION ... *the act of deceiving; a fraud or a sham*

Read: Mark 14:43-50

Key Verse: Mark 14:44 – *Judas had told them, "You will know which one to arrest when I go over and greet him easily."*

Shaq – Jordan – Bird – Magic – In the basketball community, sometimes all that's needed to be said is just one name. These names and their game transcend the necessity for a last name. In most cases, it's beyond personality, advertisement, or Madison Avenue. Without their skills or marketability their famous name wouldn't even matter. By combining those skills with their personality and popularity, they are known even by novice basketball fans.

Sometimes a one-name moniker is associated with something negative. When you mention the name of Judas, it's usually attached with betrayal, greed, and deception. It's not a very flattering way to be remembered. In the Scriptures, that's what is recorded. Why? Because of the choice Judas made to betray Jesus. He could have walked away from those who conspired against Jesus. Doing so would have given someone else the dubious honor of being a part of negative history. However, Scripture had to be fulfilled.

Judas' deception was one of the lowest actions a human being could stoop to – he betrayed his friend, the Son of God, in such a way that it lead to His death. He negotiated a payday for himself of thirty pieces of silver. Scripture says that what he was doing was pre-meditated; therefore, he should have thought out his actions more thoroughly. We must also understand the consequences of his actions and choose differently.

Deception and dishonesty from within the coaching ranks can be crippling in so many ways and thus should not be tolerated. The stories of academic fraud, cheating, and recruiting violations are running rampant.

There is only one way to live and to conduct business, and that's with honestly and integrity. The level of trust that is placed in a coach by the parents, the players, the administration, and the basketball community cannot be poisoned with decisions that can lead to the destruction of relationships or programs.

THE COACHES' CORNER

QUESTION AND ANSWER SESSION FEATURING:

Robert Dinardo, Head Women's Basketball Coach, Concordia College, NY

Gerald Davis: Suppose a recruit asks you about playing time; some coaches will tell a recruit what he wants to hear. What is your response when it comes to trying to secure the services of that recruit?

Robert Dinardo: If a girl I'm recruiting asks about playing time, I try to be as absolutely honest as possible. If a girl isn't going to play much, I tell her that. If she's going to play, I say that too, but I *never* promise a player that she will start. If she does wind up being a starter then she feels great, and if she doesn't then she doesn't feel like she was lied to.

Gerald Davis: Give me your top five reasons for why it's best to tell a recruit the truth.

Robert Dinardo:

- Honesty is the best policy to follow, period.
- A player will never feel betrayed if you do what you say you're going to do.
- Honesty builds trust, and a player who trusts you will always go the extra mile for you.
- Players who trust you will communicate that to future recruits.
- A reputation of honesty is great for any program.

3-POINTERS

Mark 13:22 (KJV) – For false Christ and false prophets shall rise, and show signs and wonders, to seduce, if it were possible, even the elect.

Luke 8:16-17 (KJV) – No man, when he hath lighted a candle, covereth it with a vessel, or putteth it under a bed; but setteth it on a candlestick, that they which enter in may see the light. For nothing is secret that shall be made manifest; neither anything hid, that shall not be known and come abroad.

Genesis 27:35 – And he said, "Your brother came deceitfully and has taken away your blessing.

BUZZER BEATER

Every man has three men to deal with: the man he thinks others see; the man he thinks he is; the man he really is.

- Edwin Louis Cole

POST-GAME NOTES

....
....
....
....
....
....
....

REBELLION ... *resistance against any power or restriction*

Read: Numbers 16:1-22

Key Verse: Numbers 16:3 – *They went to Moses and Aaron and said, "We have had enough of your presumption; you are no better than anyone else; everyone in Israel has been chosen of the Lord, and he is with all of us. What right do you have to put yourselves forward, claiming that we must obey you, and acting as though you were greater than anyone else among all these people of the Lord?"*

Unfortunately, I have witnessed a coaching colleague (a good coach and a good person, with a winning record) lose his job when some top players in his program rebelled against his leadership. They took their complaints to the athletic director, who adhered to their demands. My friend was unceremoniously retired from his position. When I asked what prompted the uprising, he was unaware of their concerns and problems. He was totally caught "off-guard" and felt as if his best friend had just shot him in the back. This situation was traumatic for all parties involved. However, it could and should have been avoided if only the lines of communication had been open, if loyalty was in place, and if "the chain of command process" was truly understood.

If anyone could tell you about the hardships of leading people, it would have to be Moses. It seemed as if verbal rumblings and rebellion were constant themes among the Israelites he was leading.

In one particular case, Korah, a Levite, served as a special assistant in the daily functions of the Tabernacle. He was outspoken in his displeasure of how things were going under Moses' leadership. First, he questioned who had placed Moses in his present position and why. Secondly, he stated that any Israelite who had traveled with Moses was a "chosen person" and thus there was no need to obey Moses. Both insinuations dripped with sarcasm and disrespect. His proclamations were construed and twisted to validate his own distorted beliefs.

As a coach you may have some players who will question your authority. Even so, never waver in what you believe. Always listen to the voice of the Holy Spirit. He will never lead you on the wrong path!

By the way, within a matter of months my coaching friend not only landed on his feet with another coaching position but it was a better one at that. Isn't that just like God? He can turn any negative situation into a positive one.

THE COACHES' CORNER

QUESTION AND ANSWER SESSION FEATURING:

Andy Stampfel, Head Men's Basketball Coach, The City College of New York, NY

Gerald Davis: Can you remember cutting or releasing a player because of their negative influence on the team?

Andy Stampfel: There have been some guys who've thought they were better than they were, weren't getting the minutes they thought they should be getting, and their bad attitude was creating a negative environment around the team. So, see ya!

Gerald Davis: Has a player ever openly disobeyed a direct order or even refused to run a play? If so, how did you handle the situation?

Andy Stampfel: Those are usually isolated instances, so we just do some damage control. I have only had one time where it really never got any better and actually got worse. That was last year, and I had to let that player go.

3-POINTERS

Numbers 16:41 (NASB) – *But on the next day all the congregation of the sons of Israel grumbled against Moses and Aaron, saying, "you are the ones who have caused the death of the Lord's people.*

Joshua 24:15 (KJV) – *And if it seem evil unto you to serve the Lord, choose you this day whom ye will serve; whether the gods which your fathers served that were on the other side of the flood, or the gods of the Amorites, in whose land ye dwell: but as for me and my house, we will serve the Lord.*

1 Samuel 15:23 – *For rebellion is as the sin of divination, and insubordination is as iniquity and idolatry. Because you have rejected the word of the Lord, He has also rejected you from being king.*

BUZZER BEATER

The beginning of men's rebellion against God was, and is, the lack of a thankful heart.

- Francis Schaeffer

POST-GAME NOTES

....
....
....
....
....
....
....

SELFISHNESS ... *showing care solely or primarily for oneself*

Read: Matthew 18:1-6

Key Verse: Matthew 18:4 – *Therefore anyone who humbles himself as this little child is the greatest in the Kingdom of Heaven.*

A "nut" in basketball terms is not your ordinary nut. It's not a peanut, a walnut, or an almond. In the world of basketball, the word "nut" describes an individual whose basketball play and tendencies can be categorized as selfish.

Selfishness in basketball or any sport can be destructive. It tears away the inner fabric of a team, especially emotionally. Imagine this ... your team is on a 3 on 2 fast break, which in the end results in a 20-foot fade away jumper. The ultimate goal in that situation of course is a lay-up or dunk. When selfishness raises its ugly head, and the only thing on the mind of the player is, "I gotta get mine," needless to say, that kind of shot-selection or mindset set cannot produce winners or a winning program.

THE COACHES' CORNER

QUESTION AND ANSWER SESSION FEATURING:

Joe Gugliero, Girl's Basketball Coach, Long Island, NY

... and ...

Robert Mitchell, Girl's Basketball Coach, Instructor, Long Island, NY

Gerald Davis: How do you change the attitude of a selfish ball player?
Joe Gugliero:
- Clearly define their role on the team
- Set specific team-related goals for them to accomplish.

- Preach. Cite examples of prominent players (e.g., Jordan) who did not achieve true individual success until they gave themselves to their teams. When you give up self you actually grow!! If you want more for yourself give more to others. It's a universal law that applies to all aspects of life.
- Sit her on the bench.

Robert Mitchell: It is the head coach's job as well as the coaching staff to convince a selfish player that the overall goal of the team is to win. Sharing the ball on offense, making the extra pass to a teammate who has a better shot, not freezing teammates out of the action, helping on defense, taking a charge – all of these and more **must be emphasized during practice,** and you must be willing to have a consequence your players will face if your instructions are not adhered to. I have found something that has a really positive effect: asking our players (usually team captains) to police their selfish teammates by getting in their grill when they exhibit selfish tendencies.

Gerald Davis: In regards to being unselfish, what gets you more excited, a player taking a charge or a player handing out an assist?

Joe Gugliero: The charge involves one person giving herself up in a one-on-one dual with an opponent. The assist involves two people working together toward a common goal.

Actually, more often than not it involves three … no one talks about the pass that leads to the assist! Both are vitally important, but I am personally tickled by the assist. Basketball is at its most beautiful when players work together.

Robert Mitchell: This is a great question! I have to say **both.** As a firm proponent of **"share the ball – defend the ball,"** I cannot in good conscience choose one over the other. If I have a team full of players who will do both, my chances of success rise exponentially.

Gerald Davis: If I had to name one aspect of the game that I cannot tolerate it would be selfishness; what's yours?

Joe Gugliero: I have a tough time with kids who are unwilling to learn and refuse to do things in a different way. A coach is first and foremost a teacher. Coaches devise and adopt systems, teach techniques, and develop strategies. Kids, particularly talented kids who are unwilling and/or reluctant to learn, can cripple teams.

Unfortunately we see more and more of this type of phenomenon in the game today with "role models" leading the charge towards anarchy. Please refer to the Larry Brown firing from the New York Knicks for illustrative purposes.

Robert Mitchell: I would tend to agree with you. Selfishness leads to what I call "personal agenda," which is a cancer to any team. A perfect example is the following: there are less than 15 seconds left in a game, the team is down by 3 ... during a time-out the coach calls for a play to inbound the ball, drive, and then kick it out to one of our perimeter shooters. The play is executed to perfection but ends up in the hands of the worst outside shooter on the floor. She starts to drive to the basket and pulls up and takes a questionable shot and misses badly. Her teammate is wide open on the perimeter waiting for the pass that never came. After fouling the other team (who secured the rebound) and calling a time-out, the coach took the player to the side and pointed out the poor decision making on this player's part and that it was her job to get the ball to her teammate who was in a better position.

3-POINTERS

Philippians 2:3-4 (KJV) – *Let nothing be done through strife or vainglory; but in lowliness of mind let each esteem other better than themselves. Look not every man on his own things, but every man also on the things of other.*

Luke 9:23 (KJV) – *And he said to them all, if any man will come after me, let him deny himself, and take up his cross daily, and follow me.*

Mark 8:36 (KJV) – *For what shall it profit a man, if he shall gain the whole world, and lose his own soul?*

BUZZER BEATER

A man is called selfish *not* for pursuing his own good, but for neglecting his neighbor's.

- Richard Whately

POST-GAME NOTES

....

....

....

....

....

....

....

ABOUT THE AUTHOR
Gerald T. Davis

I accepted Jesus Christ as my personal Lord and Savior while I was in high school. I was married for 24 wonderful years to Digna M. Davis until she graduated to glory after fighting valiantly against cancer.

I have three children – Christina, Bryan, and Brandon (twins), and one grandson, Jeremiah T. Davis.

I am a member of Christian Cultural Center in Brooklyn, New York, and I have coached men's and women's basketball on the high school level, college level, JUCO, and AAU – and I love every minute of it!

Printed in the United States
136129LV00002B/2/P

9 781606 477823